D0802957

THE FABER BOOK OF
20TH-CENTURY ITALIAN POEMS

also by Jamie McKendrick

THE SIROCCO ROOM
THE KIOSK ON THE BRINK
THE MARBLE FLY
SKY NAILS: POEMS 1979–1997
INK STONE

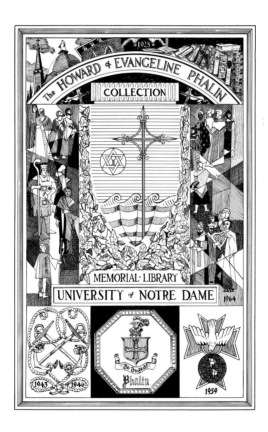

THE FABER BOOK OF
20th-Century Italian Poems

edited by
JAMIE McKENDRICK

faber and faber

First published in 2004
by Faber and Faber Limited
3 Queen Square London WC1N 3AU
Published in the United States by Faber and Faber Inc.
an affiliate of Farrar Straus and Giroux LLC, New York

Photoset by RefineCatch Ltd, Bungay, Suffolk
Printed in England by T. J. International Ltd, Padstow, Cornwall

All rights reserved
Introduction and selection © Jamie McKendrick, 2004
Copyright in individual poems remains the property of the translators

The right of Jamie McKendrick to be identified as editor
of this work has been asserted in accordance with Section 77
of the Copyright, Designs and Patents Act 1988

*This book is sold subject to the condition that it shall not,
by way of trade or otherwise, be lent, resold, hired out
or otherwise circulated without the publisher's prior consent
in any form of binding or cover other than that
in which it is published and without a similar condition
including this condition being imposed on the subsequent purchaser*

A CIP record for this book
is available from the British Library

ISBN 0-571-19700-0

2 4 6 8 10 9 7 5 3 1

Contents

Introduction

Twentieth-century Italian poetry is still largely known in the English-speaking world via Montale, who has held the same kind of sway, both within his culture and internationally, that T. S. Eliot did. From the earlier part of the century, Quasimodo (another Nobel Prize-winner) and Ungaretti will be known to the more interested, and D'Annunzio has acquired a kind of infamy. Over the last fifteen years some welcome breaches have been made in this state of incuriosity with the book publication of translations of, among others, Gozzano, Bertolucci, Fortini, Sereni, Levi, Penna and Cattafi, but these have mostly enjoyed restricted circulation and little critical notice. There are signs of an awakening interest in more recent poetry, especially in the U.S., with the publication of anthologies and of books by two younger poets, Buffoni and Magrelli. In the meantime, the emphasis on Montale has if anything intensified.

An anthology like this one, of some hundred and fifty poems, including less than fifty poets, to represent a hundred years of poetry, may seem to have little chance of effecting a shift of opinion, and may even, despite its intentions, confirm the prevailing view. Montale translations offer an embarrassment of riches for the anthologist as the many recent books demonstrate, whilst public interest in other poets has hardly ever extended so far as to admit alternative versions, at least in book form. It isn't my intention to challenge Montale's status, and predictably Montale, Ungaretti and Saba are the poets most fully represented. Still, my hope is that even within its small compass this anthology may offer the reader more than a glimpse, beyond the eminence of these poets, of the great variety and vitality of the poetry of their contemporaries and successors.

Italy's poetry has been marked by the turbulent political history of the century – the two world wars with the rise of Fascism between them; a deeply divided post-war state: divided geographically between the largely rural and impoverished south and the relatively well-heeled and industrial north, and divided politically between the Christian Democrats and the Communists. The fragility of this state, with acts of murder both 'red' and 'black', has laid an unavoidable burden of conscience on the language of its poets and writers. An analogy with the poets of Northern Ireland from the Seventies onwards is very approximate but still relevant. The political conflicts were of a different nature but the responses of the poets were not altogether dissimilar. Comparable too is the sense in which political division and sectarianism can engender in writers an interior debate, an enriched kind of *coscienza*, with its dual meaning of conscience and consciousness. A century whose onset is dominated by D'Annunzio's flamboyant aestheticism, and which declines into the brash posturing of Futurism, is set up for a fall. In Ungaretti's poems from the First World War a Modernist technique of fragments and lacunae is both a testing- and an emptying-out of the accumulated rhetoric of this tradition. Montale, also a combatant (though from his poems you would hardly guess it), and a poet likewise immersed in the work of D'Annunzio, retains more of the traditional poetic forms but they are shadowed by an equally extreme *rifiuto*, a refusal, as he himself declared, to be conscripted by 'any kind of clerisy, whether red or black'. It's no coincidence that over fifty of the poems in his opus begin with a negative construction and one of his most celebrated 'manifesto' poems ends with the lines: 'Codesto solo oggi possiamo dirti,/ ciò che *non* vogliamo, ciò che *non* siamo' (Today we can only tell you/ what we don't want, what we are not).

Italian poetry has as many different schools and factions as its politics has parties – I Crepusculari, Hermeticism, Gruppo 63, I Novissimi, etc. – but there is also a sense of an ongoing conversation, sometimes a bitter quarrel, between its poets. The poetry of the so-called *terza generazione* – of poets like Pasolini, Fortini and to an extent Cattafi – shows signs of explicit argument and political *impegno* (commitment). A civic awareness informs even those poets who appear to have retired from the fray, such as Sereni, who speaks in bitter, almost posthumous tones from the enforced margin as a prisoner of war in Algeria, or Bertolucci, writing of his beloved Parma countryside. This context makes a striking exception of Penna, for whose unwaveringly narrow focus any politics would seem to be an anathema, and for whom class might only represent another erotic opportunity.

At various points in compiling this anthology, that negative credo of Montale's sprang to mind. What this book isn't is a fair and representative survey of Italian poetry, nor does it claim to include the best Italian poems of the period – though on both counts it doesn't score too badly. There are a number of significant poets, and some important poems, that are not included, with a few tormenting omissions. Longer poems have had to be excluded for reasons of space, though in a few instances I have included excerpts.

What this anthology wants, and wants to be, is harder to explain. It's both a personal gathering as well as a collection that I hope works sufficiently well in English to give at least an idea of the breadth and complexity of Italian poetry in this period. Although I have also been unable to include anything of the flourishing tradition of dialect poetry, except in the case of Zanzotto, I hope that it will at least reflect some of the many Italies, the regional particularities and diversities: Saba's Trieste with its lingering Slavic and Austro-Hungarian traces; the Sicilies of Quasimodo, Cattafi and Ripellino, mythic, menacing and baroque respectively; Bertolucci's Parma; Sinisgalli's *Mezzogiorno*, and so on. Like Montale, who left his coastal Liguria for what he called the *terra firma* of culture in Florence and later Milan, many of these poets have been associated with 'metropolitan' (Florentine, Milanese and Roman) literary groupings and factions but they have brought with them a kind of *sfondo*, an irreducible background that colours their perspective, and sometimes even their language.

We're accustomed to think of provincialism in negative terms, but many of these poets explore an attachment to place that is neither excluding nor small-minded, and like Bertolucci who writes feelingly of a passeggiata – 'the pace is slow and easy, that of the provinces' – are apt to discover something Edenic in the sticks. After all, many small provincial Italian towns have been cultural centres for centuries. Rather than the closure of provincialism, twentieth-century Italian poetry offers many cosmopolitan perspectives, for example in Ungaretti's Egypt and France, Montale's Vienna and Eastbourne, or in several other poets' evocations of abroad. As regards religion, the Vatican is a presence in Pasolini and Sinisgalli, but also the Judaic heritage can be felt in poets such as Saba, Fortini, Levi, Bassani, Rosselli, Ombres and Anedda.

How robust these distinctive, still un-unified Italies will be in the face of the current homogenizing and media-driven politics remains to be seen. (Their advent was already foreseen by poets like Pasolini and Risi.) A feature of the most recent generation of poets, here only thinly represented, is if anything more attuned to a crisis with global repercussions. Anedda's Sardinia is literally undermined by American submarines, her 'nights of Western peace' are shot through with intimations of war, and Magrelli is able to hear a concealed ultimatum in 'the music of the West'. Written in the early Nineties, the image of the earth as a hi-jacked plane in his poem 'Aperçu' has already been confirmed for us in its urgency and alarm.

I also hope that the choice of poems will help establish something of the context, the culture if you like, out of which the poetry has arisen: the text versus text, the tributes, the quarrels, affectionate or otherwise, that have animated the poems. Although it risks overstressing the 'literary' and intertextual nature of Italian poetry, this choice of poems which argue with or make reference to other poems and poets is a notable feature, and goes along with a more self-reflexive and philosophical cast to the writing than is common within the Anglo-Saxon tradition. Because allusion is notoriously hard to translate, this sense of an ongoing conversation is unlikely to be fully perceptible to an English reader. Through translation, will the reader hear that the ending of Montale's 'My Muse' (È la sola musica che supporto') is echoing a phrase from a Sereni poem which closes with the sound of tents flapping on poles: 'Non è musica d'angeli, è la mia/ sola musica e mi basta'? I have tried in the selection of these poems to bring some of this play above the threshold of the audible. For instance, Orelli's 'Rhine Eels', which at first seems a straightforward, even blunt, descriptive poem, can also be read as a reply poem to Montale's 'Eel', playing the brutal actuality of his fish-stall against its famously symbolizing forebear. This poem also provides other examples of what gets lost in translation – the way the language is layered with allusion. The phrase 'ed è subito calmo' (and it is suddenly calm – here translated as 'but soon it's all over') immediately suggests Quasimodo's famous three-line drawing-down of the blinds which ends 'Ed è subito sera' ('And it's suddenly evening'). The word 'guizzo' (dart, flash) recalls Montale's use of the word in his 'The Eel': 'una luce scoccata dai castagni/ ne accende il guizzo in pozze d'acquamorte'. Behind both uses there is the ghostly presence of Dante's Geryon, the image of Fraud, who is described as moving 'come anguilla' (like an eel) and earlier:

> Nel vano tutta sua coda *guizzava*,
>   torcendo in su la velenosa forca
>   ch'a *guisa* di scorpion la punta armava . . .
>   (*Inferno*, XVII, 1.25–27)

(In Steve Ellis's translation: 'He darted his tail about in the air,/ twisting up the poisonous/ fork that arms its tip, like a scorpion's'.) Even Montale's reference to 'acquamorta' (stagnant or 'dead' water) inevitably evokes Quasimodo's famous poem of that name. This eelish skein of allusions could be endlessly unwound, but what I want to suggest here is both the densely intertextual nature of Italian poetry and the way translation has to make do with less – or else find its own cultural equivalents to give some resonance to the language.

Where possible I have chosen more than one, occasionally several, translators for each poet so as to give a less monovocal sense of the work. The translators have added their own voices to this conversation, and though the nature of anthologies unavoidably tends towards excerpts and ellipses, I believe that as well as the speech some of the different music, of the tent-poles as well as the angels, can be heard beyond Italy's linguistic borders.

Preface

Personal taste, the availability of translations and the perceived standing of the individual poets have all shaped the making of this book. Except in the case of the better known poets, however, there has been little attempt at proportional representation: the number of poems allocated to each poet does not necessarily indicate either a personal preference or a judgement upon the poet's importance.

I am indebted to all of the translators here included, especially to those who have responded with requested poems. For advice and help of various kinds, I am very grateful to Federico Bonaddio, Simon Carnell, Luca Guerneri, Clara Caleo Green, Peter Hainsworth, Michael Hofmann, Tom Lubbock, Michael O'Neill, Tom Paulin, Pawel Pawlikovsky, Xon de Ros, Erica Segre, Ornella Tarantola, Stella Tillyard and Fiona Whitehouse. I would also like to thank Christopher Reid, then poetry editor at Faber, who conceived the idea, and Paul Keegan, the present editor, who has seen it through with patience and expertise. My thanks also to Matthew Hollis and Charles Boyle at Faber.

J. McK.

2OTH-CENTURY ITALIAN POEMS

GABRIELE D'ANNUNZIO

[*1863–1936; b. Pescara, Abruzzi*]

The Shepherds

September – let's be off. Time to migrate.
Up there in the Abruzzi now my shepherds
are leaving the folds and moving to the sea,
climbing down to the savage Adriatic –
which is green like the pastures in the mountains.

They have drunk deeply at the Alpine fountains,
hoping to make a taste of that home water
stay in their exiled hearts to comfort them,
and on the way for miles deceive their thirst.
They've cut themselves new rods of hazelwood.

They drop to the plain by the old droving road,
as if along a silent river of grass,
treading the footprints of their ancestors.
O hear the cry of the first to recognise
the shimmering of the sea against the beach!

And now the flock is walking down a reach
of shoreline. Nothing changes in the air.
The sun is fading all that living wool
until it looks the colour of the sand.
Rinsing of water, trampling feet, sweet sounds.

Ah why am I not there among my shepherds?

Alistair Elliot

The Mouth of the Arno

The mouth of woman never was to me
so full of pleasure in the ways of love
(excepting yours, excepting yours, right now)
as the pale opening out, the silent lips
of this small stream that springs in Falterona.
What woman can abandon
herself (excepting only you) so sweetly
as this appeased and sated current does?
It does not sing
and yet it flows like melody towards
its bitter end.

    The nature of its beauty
    I cannot speak,
    being like one who hears
    sounds that pierce his sleep, and unknown
      powers
    enter his sleeping mind.

Leaping a little to meet it the green waves
burst into confident foam,
the graceful surging of young animals.
They move with greater bounds
of joy than Donatello's hand-in-hand
cherubs in marble warm beneath the chisel
when he was decorating white cathedrals.
Under the swags and chains of flowers and fruits
those children wreath around his balustrades,
skipping and turning; but their dance is never
as wild as this one.

    Does any other creature
    live with such grace

and in such perfect joy? –
except for Dante's lark up there
that goes for walks on air.

Perhaps my soul when it has thrown itself
deep in its state of song and sees its glory,
perhaps your soul when it has thrown itself
deep into love and so forgets the history
of the illusions it was trapped among
and strains with me toward high victory –
perhaps we shall experience the full
happiness of the free
overlapping wave, the strong unfolded wings
and the untamed expansion of its song.
Keep watch, and worship.

      Keep praying, watch with awe.
      You see? Your bare
      feet have left prints of light,
      and before your eyes wonders are rising
      out of the water. See?

Great flower-cups, chalices, rise from the pouring water,
woven somehow like mail from finest gold.
The clouds the hills the woods the shores the waters
are visible through the enormous flower-heads,
you see? – far-off, transparent
as unknown countries that appear in dreams.
Butterflies golden as your open hands
flying in pairs discover on the waters
with wonder those great blossoms that seem foreign,
while you breathe in
the smell of salt.

      The long hand of the sun
      plays its divine game

with shifting shades of joy,
like the iridescent throats of pigeons
lifting, swollen with song.

This vision is the fishermen's hanging nets.
Some hang like parts of balances slung from spars
propped up on the high platforms which jut out
where men can sit and watch and pull the rope;
others are hung over the bows of dories,
and cut the eternal mirror
of passing water that reflects them; when the sun
beats on the boats from astern and the oars stand
at rest, a burst of radiance transforms them:
great chalices, flower-cups, rise from the pouring waters,
lilies of fire.

The young face of the sun
plays its divine game,
which lasts no longer than
the song of pigeons. Enjoy enchantment,
our single soul: worship here.

Alistair Elliot

The Seahorse
(after D'Annunzio)

Supple muse or willow wand,
lean as a greyhound–

your finest fodder a handful of biting salt.
As avid for it as a snub-nosed goat.

But gentle as with neck inclined
you feed on seaweed from a Siren's hand.

Simon Carnell

CORRADO GOVONI
[1884–1965; b. Tamara, Ferrara]

The Tapping

Who is down there, what doctor
in the field of flowering hemp,
listening, one by one, to all the trees?

In the tapping of his hammer one seems to hear
the work of some fantastic carpenter
whose all-day job is the nailing up of biers,
and at such a frenzied pace. Alone, out there,
amid the litter of the hemp and straw,
he stops from time to time, and bending low
as if in pain, breaks into a mad run,
and a guffaw of vile, funereal derision.

Felix Stefanile

Field and Clouds

Just now, the rain-storm spent,
the green plain gives off
a fragrance of cool mint.
There's still the steady trickling of the water
slowly, drop by drop,
down quivering stalks of grass,
rosy eye-lids of flowers.
Far off, where the sky glows,
the grand and blue-enamelled watering can
with the bright handle, of the rainbow.

Felix Stefanile

GUIDO GOZZANO
[*1883–1916; b. Turin*]

Eulogy of Ancillary Amours

I

I seize upon that nimble servant who
is always full of gossip, on the go
as intermediary between us two.

I'm stirred by her fresh laughter, by the slow
waiting in vain, her sharp remarks, the hour,
the scent of something from Boccaccio . . .

She likes to mock, to struggle, to implore,
she even brings her mistress into play:
'How shameful it would be for her! My poor,

poor mistress! . . .' And she gives herself to me.

II

Like figures out of the *Decameron*,
maidservants give us, and without torment,
more healthy pleasure than the mistress can.

Not the shrewd pain the lady hard as flint
inflicts, not slow and sickly martyrdom,
and not the sort of tedious sentiment

which makes night long ('Oh, will sleep never come?'),
not, above all, the soul made sad by pleasure:
a calmer, much more masculine good time.

I praise the love of maidservants for ever!

J. G. Nichols

Cocotte

Again I've seen our garden, and the one
next door, the palmtrees standing by the road,
and the rough railings from whose other side
she gave a sugared almond . . .

II

                             'Little one,
what is that game you're playing, all alone?'
'I'm playing at the Universal Flood.'

I showed my bucket, and the oddities
modelled in sand to adorn my little stage;
and she bent down as though she felt an urge
to kiss me with an impulse to reverse
the action, to withdraw; and through the bars
she kissed me like a bird inside a cage.

Her charming face will stay with me, I know,
seen from behind square bars, throughout my life!
She seized my head as though she were a thief;
I was amazed to find myself held so,
so closely held, her face and mouth close to,
so very different from my mother's mouth!

'You like the look of me then, little one?
You've come here for the bathing? That house there?'
'Yes . . . Here are Mummy and Daddy over here.'
She let me go at once; her face took on
a dreamy look (I realised later on)

[9]

a dream of motherhood and of despair . . .
'She's a cocotte! . . .'

                          'Mummy, what does that mean?'
'It means the lady is a wicked one:
you mustn't ever talk to her again!'

The clucking sound of that Parisian
title – co-co-tte – loaded my childish brain
with silly notions of an egg and hen . . .

I thought of all the fabled deities:
the sailors sailing for the Happy Isles . . .
Co-co-tte . . . Bad fairies with their evil spells
concealed in food and drink . . . Though no one says
what kind they are, I know their wicked ways,
the way they practise their mysterious skills!

III

One day – days later – she called out to me
behind the bars (verbena was in flower):
'You do not seem to like me any more! . . .'
'You're really a cocotte then, as they say?'
She kissed me, laughing rather desperately;
her eyes were full of melancholia.

IV

Among the disappointments, the dead joys,
twenty years on, your smile comes back today . . .
Where are you, wicked lady? Can you be
alive? How do you hide from prying eyes
(for you it were much better not to be!)
the terrible descent of all the years?

Now that the rouge is very little use,
the hair-dye, and the lipstick, and the powder,
your room stands empty of your final lover . . .
Except that one – the little elf or nis
you gave a sugared almond and a kiss –
twenty years on contrives to rediscover

you in his dream, and loves you in his dream,
and says: From my pure childhood, from that morning
perhaps I've loved but you alone, my darling!
Perhaps but you alone! I'm calling. Come!
If you should ever read these verses, come
back to the one who waits for you, my darling!

What matter now if you are not the same?
I am not four years old. I now desire
you dressed in time! It's now that I require
your past! I'll make you beautiful again –
Carlotta, Graziella are the same –
as all the ladies of my dreaming are.

My dream is nourished by the letting-go
and the regret. I love the roses that
I did not pick. What do I love but what
might well have come about but didn't? . . . So
I see the roses and the house and that
garden brought back from twenty years ago!

Your garden, still unchanged behind the bars,
among Ligurian eucalyptus still
stretches away . . . Come to the sated soul.
If I may see again that face the years
have ruined, I shall kiss that face of yours
until your mouth is once more beautiful.

If you should come, 'twould be as if you came
to bring me back myself as I was then.
The lady and the child will talk again.
We shall arise from the abyss of time.
If you should come, 'twould be as if I came
to bring you back yourself, young once again.

J. G. Nichols

The Good Companion

It was not Love, no. But our senses were
becoming curious . . . And our cultivation
of dream was such . . . We thought the rapid action
certain to gather mystery more and more.

But after your last kiss, in which I wore
out my last kiss, after my last pulsation,
I only heard dry sobbing agitation
muffled in your abundant head of hair.

Hopeless to try to melt and fuse in one
two hearts dreaming and thought had petrified;
Love cannot hold equalities together.

No sentiment. We must become immune,
and stride more strongly out along the road,
allies and good companions, and for ever.

J. G. Nichols

The Colloquies

I

These *Colloquies* . . . Now sound of body and mind,
he groups his verses and he alters them,
weighing the manuscript with even hand.

– A bit of fun with syllables and rhyme:
is this what stays of my so fleeting spring?
Is it all really here, my youthful prime?

Better be silent, calmly vanishing
now while my garden still shows signs of life,
and envy still is unprovoked to sting.

Better upon life's road to stop for breath,
now while the world to my inexpert Muse –
an actress sadly singing of her youth –

holds out a helping hand or gives applause.

II

This Muse of mine's no actress full of years
who paints her face and goes on like a child,
however much the mob derides and jeers;

young she will hold her tongue, still undefiled
by Time, like that Contessa Castiglione,
so beautiful, of whom such tales are told.

Who, finding her spring day not quite so sunny,
her youth begin to fade, sealed up the doors,
and stayed a sort of prisoner with only

Time for companion, waiting for the years
in rooms with tattered hangings, mirrorless,
hiding from common folk and courtiers

her decadence, the ultimate disgrace.

III

As for my image, I want it to stay
twenty, as in a portrait, never altered;
my friends, you will not see me on my way

bent by the years and tremulous and battered!
In this my silence I shall stay the friend
who was so dear to you, a touch dim-witted;

I'll be that youngster still, old-fashioned, fond,
who sighed with longing in the light of stars,
Artur and Friedrich always on his mind,

and yet forsook rebel philosophers
to give the swallow its due sepulchre
or reach a blade of grass towards the claws

of topsyturvy coleoptera . . .

J. G. Nichols

FILIPPO TOMMASO MARINETTI

[*1876–1944; b. Alexandria, Egypt*]

The Futurist Aviator Speaks to His Father, Vulcan

I come to you, Vulcan, to give back the laugh
to you, sputtering, old ventriloquist.
Believe me, I'm out of your reach!
You'd snare me if you could,
in your coils of lava,
that luck you have with foolish dreamers
who climb your slopes
when the hypnotizing sadness of your monolithic sunsets
convulses into horrid, titanic guffaws,
and sometimes an earthquake.
I fear neither omens, nor menace of the abyss
that at your whim can bury a city
beneath a tumulus of ore and ash and blood.
I am the Futurist, strong and indomitable,
hauling aloft my wild and enduring heart:
and so it is I sit me down at Aurora's board,
and feast upon her color-show of fruits;
or trample meridians, launch my bombs,
pursue the fleeing armies of the sunset,
dragging the wistful, sighing twilight
in tow behind me.

Etna, Etna, who dances better than I
pirouetting above your fearsome maw
bellowing a thousand meters below?
Watch me descend and dip toward your sulphurous breath
and dart between your columns of reddening clouds
to listen to the rumbling of that vast belly,

your heaving, gulping, deafening landslide,
your war at the center of the earth.
In vain your carbon rage
that would buffet me back to the sky!
I grip the flight-stick firmly in my hands . . .

I enter now, through the wide gap of your mouth,
a sprawl of peaks,
and drop still further down
to inspect your monstrous gums . . .
Vulcan! what weeds are these
limp plumes of smoke
you nibble at,
like an ogre's blue moustache? . . .

Felix Stefanile

GESUALDO MANZELLA-FRONTINI
[1885–1957; b. Catania, Sicily]

The Anatomy Room

Perfumed autumn of amaryllises
acrid odor of phenic acid:
the anatomy room revealed
in the dwindling light of vesper-time all violet and
    gold.
Sprawled, lopsided cadavers
on stained and clotted tables.
An old man, eyes popping,
chest caved-in,
and over the jelly of his doomed eyes
the flies, unpunished,
contentedly buzzing.
Sheet of a newspaper –
the worldly note –
stuffed into the fetid mouth
of a consumptive
being measured by the deft track of the scalpel.
The sternum gives,
the bright and ruined lungs
wheeze
under pressure.
On the last table,
in shadow,
a woman split in half from the hips,
beneath the thin and rigid breasts
the belly oozing:
ah why, why, excellent creature,
surprise of my vision,

do I dandle myself before you, in the glossy whiteness
of your limbs,
a voyeur of the sudden freshness
of your vain and chaste beauty?

Felix Stefanile

DINO CAMPANA

[*1885–1932; b. Marradi, Florence*]

Woman from Genoa

You brought me a little seaweed
In your hair and a scent of wind
That came from afar and arrives weighted
With warmth on your bronzed body:
– Oh the divine
Artlessness of your slim figure –
Not love not agony, a ghost,
A shade of necessity that wanders
Serenely and ineluctably into the soul
And dissolves it in joy, in serene enchantment
So that the sirocco may carry it
Into infinity.
How small the world is and light in your hands!

Isadore Saloman

Whore with Iron-gray Eyes

With your small brutal eyes
You look at me, say nothing, wait, then draw close,
Look at me again and say nothing. Your dull
And lumpish flesh sleeps benumbed
In primordial dreams. Prostitute . . .
Who called you to life? Where do you come from?
Arid Tyrrhenian ports,
Resounding Tuscan fairs
Or under siroccos was your mother
Rolled over on the burning sand?

Hugeness impressed stupor upon you
In the feral face of a sphinx
The swarming breath of life
Tragically shakes your black mane
As if you were a she-lion
And you look at the profane blond angel
Who loves you not and you love not and who suffers
Because of you and who, tired, kisses you.

Isadore Saloman

A Siren

(*after Saba*)

Anyone watching you in the water would think: 'A siren!'
Winner in the women's swimming event, you seem
strange on the screen of my inglorious life.
While you smile in triumph I tie a thread,
a thin unbreakable thing, to your toe
but you stride past without noticing me.
Your friends, young like yourself, crowd round
and make a noise in the bar; and then
just for a moment cloud-shadow, a grave
motherly shadow shivers down from your
eyebrows to the proud, beautiful chin

and joins your rising to my own setting sun.

Derek Mahon

Ulysses

In my youth I would sail along
The Dalmatian coast. Islands appeared
On the glassy sea, white gulls sometimes
Pausing above them, intent on prey, –
Slippery, draped in weed, emeralds
Glittering in the gold sun. When high
Tide and night extinguished them, sails
Slipped off into the deep, to leeward,
Fleeing their threat, to the no-man's land
That has become my kingdom. Harbour

Lights are lit for others. I am called
Oceanwards by my untamed spirit,
By this painful, unquenched, love of life.

Robert Chandler

Woman

When you were
a young girl you stung
like a speckled mulberry. And even
your foot was a weapon, O wild one.

You were tricky to gather.
                              Still
young, you are
still beautiful. The traces
of years, those of sorrow, they bind
our spirits, make them one. And behind
the jet black hair that I coil
in my fingers I no longer fear
your small white pointed devilish ear.

Peter Robinson

The Goat

I spoke with a goat.
It was alone in a field, tethered.
Stuffed with grass, soaked
with rain, it was bleating on.

That monotonous bleat, it answered
my own pain. I responded at first

as a joke – then because sorrow's eternal,
and speaks with one unchanging voice.
That's the voice I heard,
crying in a solitary goat.

In a goat with a Semitic face
every other hurt complained,
that of all creaturely existence.

Simon Carnell

The Pig

The swill, the flower of filth, is purified
by his instinctive hunger for it:
take it away and he shrieks like a spanked child.

But what for him is a great treat
is, to your way of thinking, a torment:
he's no inkling of why the farmer's wife
chasing the poor thing about the yard
wants him porky and well stuffed:
clueless, like the rest of the living,
as to what he's destined for
when he's reached perfection.
If you look out of his eyes, switch skins,
you can feel the knife, the cut throat scream
as the dog barks among the onlookers,
and the farmer's wife laughs in the open door.

You're the one fighting back the tears,
looking into the porker's beatific face.

Simon Carnell

Thirteenth Match

On the terrace a sparse crowd
tries to keep warm. And as the sun
ducks behind a house, the action
on the field clarifies:
red shirts chasing white shirts,
back and forth,
in a peculiar iridescent light
which keeps the night at bay.
The wind diverts the ball from its path;
Dame Fortune slips
the blindfold back over her eyes . . .

And it's good to be gathered
in a small crowd frozen
like the last men on a hill,
watching the very last game.

Simon Carnell

Caffè Tergeste

Caffè Tergeste, the delirious drunk
harangues your bright white tabletops
where I write my most joyful songs.

Café of thieves and den of whores,
I suffered agonies at your tables,
suffered to fashion myself a new heart.

I thought: when I'll have enjoyed to the full
my own death, the nothing I predict it to be,
who'll repay me then for having lived?

I'm not disposed to call myself magnanimous,
but if being born's a fault, for my greater guilt,*
I'd show more compassion to my enemy.

Lowlife café, where once I hid my face,
today I watch you with delight:
you reconcile the Italian with the Slav,

late at night, across the billiard table's baize.

Jamie McKendrick

A Memory

I cannot sleep. I see a street, some trees,
and in my heart the old anxieties gather.
We would go there alone, to be together,
another boy and me.

It was Passover, the old folks' rites arcane
and slow. And if he doesn't care enough,
I thought, and if he doesn't come tomorrow?
And tomorrow he did not come: a new pain.
Spasms, toward evening, of grief. For I now know
that friendship wasn't what we had in our grove;
what we had was love –

* This stanza is obscure but may refer to the circumstances of Saba's birth:
despite converting to Judaism before marrying, his Venetian father abandoned
Saba's Jewish, Triestine mother before he was born. It's possible that the
'greater guilt' here describes his feelings about his own birth – just as the
reconciliation between the two 'races' in the last stanza has some relevance for
the poet's own predicament. [Translator's note]

the first. And such love then, and what a glow
of joy, between the hills and sea of Trieste.
But why, tonight, am I unable to rest
when all that happened fifteen years ago?

Geoffrey Brock

February Evening

The moon appears.
                    The avenue remains
sunlit, though evening has begun to fall.
Indifferent youths will gather here,
scatter toward small aims.
                    And it's the thought
of death that helps us, after all, to live.

Geoffrey Brock

VINCENZO CARDARELLI
[*1887–1959; b. Tarquinia*]

Dawn

Only in you, dawn, is there ease
for the laboured breathing
of the death I bear with me.
Only in you is there a cure
for my insomnia, which resembles
a thunderous river,
plundering, infernal,
where, each night, I descend,
battling in vain . . .
That's when you appear,
always arriving so stealthily
you almost frighten,
and eavesdrop and spy,
most vagabond of ghosts,
white-faced dawn.
The nightmares stop,
the phantoms vanish.
Death, my gloomy
companion through the small hours,
leaves, sloping off
with the tread of a thief.
I emerge from it all
and retrieve myself
out of the dark currents;
shaken, I take refuge
in a petrified sleep.

– Dawn, charitable dawn,
sea of uncertain light,
in which everything finds a source.

Michael O'Neill

Lament

I am like Mercutio
trapped between the Capulets and Montagues:
a figure to be mocked,
a victim who did nothing wrong,
the dupe of some fate
which, full of whims and treachery,
smiles at me, in the midst of disaster,
extending dubious favours
and tempting invitations.
'Seek,' it has the nerve to tell me, 'seek to live
for the moment, and do not despair.
Each day has its allotted evil.'
Who speaks to me in this way?
Which cosmic Boss has my life in his sights?
A demon or a God?
My blighted, chance-ruled life!
I've never had a lucky break
that wasn't spliced with misfortune.
I've never tasted joy
that lacked its dose of poison.
I'm afraid of the best
since it destroys the good,
and only pin my hopes
on rotten weather.

Michael O'Neill

CAMILLO SBARBERO
[1888–1967; b. S. Maria Ligure]

'Father, even if you were not'

Father, even if you were not
my father, even if you were no relation of mine,
for your own sake I'd love you just as much.
Because I shall never forget that winter's morning
when from your window you spotted
the first violet on the wall across the way
and excitedly reported the event to us.
Then with the wooden ladder on your shoulder
you went outside and propped it against the wall.
We little ones stood at the window.

And that other occasion I remember,
when my little sister was still quite young
and you chased her threateningly around the house
(I've no idea what the headstrong girl had done).
But once you'd caught her, shrieking
from terror, you lacked the heart to follow it through:
because you'd seen yourself in pursuit
of your little daughter, and scared as she was
you hesitantly drew her to your chest,
and there with hugs and caresses
you folded her round as if to defend her
against the brute that had been the you of moments before.

Father, even if you were not
my father, even if you were no relation of mine,
of all the men in the world, and no less now
for your childlike spirit, I'd love you.

Christopher Reid

'Hush, soul. These are the abject'

Hush, soul. These are the abject
days when one must live without will,
the days of hopeless waiting.
Like a bare tree in the middle of winter,
sorry for itself in the empty courtyard,
I don't believe I shall leaf again
and doubt if I have ever done so.
Walking the streets, alone like this,
jostled and invisible,
I feel absent even to myself.
I am drawn always to the noise of the crowd,
stop, stunned, in front of shop windows
and swivel at the rustle of every skirt.
At the singing of some blind street-musician,
at the unexpected flash of a neck,
idiotic tears drop from my eyes,
my eyes are kindled with desire.
Because my whole life is in my eyes:
everything that passes stirs it
as a listless wind stirs stagnant water.
I am like a mirror, perfectly resigned
to reflecting every bit of street life.
Into myself, though, I never look,
as there's nothing to see . . .

Come evening, in my own bed,
I stretch out full length, as in a coffin.

Christopher Reid

GIUSEPPE UNGARETTI
[1888–1970; b. Alexandria, Egypt]

Agony

To die like thirsty larks
upon the mirage

Or as the quail
the sea once past
having no more
will to fly
dies in the first thickets

But not to live on lamentation
like a blinded goldfinch

Patrick Creagh

Watch

Cima Quattro, 23 December 1915

A whole night through
thrown down beside
a butchered comrade
with his clenched teeth
turned to the full moon
and the clutching
of his hands
thrust
into my silence
I have written
letters full of love

Never have I
clung
so fast to life

Patrick Creagh

I Am Alive

Valloncello di Cima Quattro, 5 August 1916

Like this stone
of Monte San Michele
as cold as this
as hard as this
as dried as this
as stubborn as this
as utterly
dispirited as this

Like this stone
is my unseen
weeping

Death
we discount
by living

Patrick Creagh

In Memoriam

Locvizza, 30 September 1916

He was called
Mohammed Sheab

Descendant of nomad emirs
a suicide
because he no longer had
a country

He loved France
and changed his name

Became Marcel
but was not French
and had forgotten how
to live
in his own people's tent
where they listen to the sing-song
of the Koran
as they sip coffee

He did not know
how to release
the song
of his unconstraint

I followed his coffin
I and the manageress of the hotel
where we lived
in Paris
number 5 rue des Carmes
steep decrepit alleyway

He rests
in the cemetery at Ivry
a suburb that always
looks
like the day
they dismantle a fairground

And perhaps only I
still know
he lived

Patrick Creagh

Levant*

The line of smoke
dies out upon
the distant ring of the sky

Clatter of heels clapping of hands
and the clarinet's shrill flourishes
and the sky is ashen
trembles gentle uneasy
like a dove

In the stern Syrian emigrants are dancing

In the bow a young man is alone

On Saturday evenings at this time
Jews
in those parts
carry away
their dead
through the shell's spiralling
uncertainties
of alleyways
of lights

* Ungaretti is leaving his birthplace of Alexandria on his way to France. 'In those parts' refers to Alexandria. [Translator's note]

Churning of water
like the racket from the stern
that I hear within the shadow
of
sleep

Patrick Creagh

My Rivers

I cleave to this mutilated tree
forsaken in this hollow
that is as lifeless
as a circus
between performances
and I watch
the clouds pass
quietly across the moon

This morning I stretched out
in an urn of water
and like a relic
rested

The Isonzo polished me
in its current
like one of its own stones

I hoisted myself
up and went
like an acrobat
over the water

I squatted down
near my clothes

foul with war
and like a bedouin
bowed down to receive
the sun

This is the Isonzo
and here I have
best known myself to be
an obedient nerve
of the universe

My torture is
not to believe myself
in harmony

But those hidden
hands that knead me
give to me
the rarest
happiness

I have reviewed
the ages
of my life

These are
my rivers

This is the Serchio*
which has given water
for two thousand years maybe
to my peasant people
to my father and my mother

* The Serchio flows near Lucca. [Translator's note]

This is the Nile
that saw me
born and growing
burning with ignorance
in the wide plains

This is the Seine
and in its turbulence
I have been stirred
and come to know myself

These are my rivers
summed up in the Isonzo

This is my nostalgia
that shines through to me
in each of them
now that it is night
that my life seems to me
a corolla
of shadows

Patrick Creagh

Chiaroscuro

Even the tombs have disappeared

Endless black expanse gone down
from this balcony
to the cemetery

It occurred to me
I'd look in on my Arab friend again
who killed himself the other evening

Day comes up

The tombs return
flattened in the dismal green
of the final darkness
and confused green
of first light

Marcus Perryman and Peter Robinson

On the Edge of Sleep

The night's violation I witness

The air is riddled
like lacework
with the cross-fire
of men
withdrawn
in trenches
like snails into their shells

It seems as though
an out of breath
swarm of stonemasons
chiseled the volcanic
cobblestones
of my streets
and I listened to it
without seeing
on the edge of sleep

Marcus Perryman and Peter Robinson

Contrite

I gang prowlin' roon'
My sheep's body
Wi' the hunger o' a wolf.

I am like
A wallowin' barge
On a tumultuous ocean.

Hugh MacDiarmid

Last Quarter

1927

Moon,
Skyfeather,
So paper-thin,
Barren,
Broadcasting the murmurs of stripped souls?

To the pale one – what ever
Will the bats in the ruined theatre,
The dreaming goats, be transmitting?
And amidst burnt leaves in the remains of the fire,
With all its crystalline outpouring,
A nightingale?

Simon Carnell and Erica Segre

The Flash of the Mouth

Thousands of men before me,
And even more freighted with years than I am,
Were wounded to the quick
By the flash of a mouth.

Knowing this won't be the thing
That lessens my suffering.

But if you look at me with mercy,
And speak to me, a music fills the air,
And I forget that the wound burns.

Andrew Frisardi

EUGENIO MONTALE

[*1896–1981; b. Genoa*]

'Don't ask us for the word to frame'

Don't ask us for the word to frame
our shapeless spirit on all sides,
and proclaim it in letters of fire to shine
like a lone crocus in a dusty field.

Ah, the man who walks secure,
a friend to others and himself,
indifferent that high summer prints
his shadow on a peeling wall!

Don't ask us for the phrase that can open worlds,
just a few gnarled syllables, dry like a branch.
This, today, is all that we can tell you:
what we are *not*, what we do *not* want.

Jonathan Galassi

from Mediterranean

[6]

We don't know if tomorrow has green pastures
in mind for us to lie down in beside
the ever-youthful patter of fresh water
or if it means to plant us in some arid
outback ugly valley of the shadow
where dayspring's lost for good, interred beneath
a lifetime of mistakes. We'll maybe wake up
in foreign cities where the sun's a ghost,

a figment of itself and angular
starched consonants braid the tongue at its root
so all sense of who we are is lost to words,
and nothing that we know can be unravelled.
Even then, some vestige of the sea,
its plosive tide, its fretwork crests will surge
inside our syllables, bronze like the chant of bees.
However far we've stumbled from the source
a trace of the sea's voice will lodge in us
as the sunlight somehow still abides in
faded tufts that cling to bricks and kerbstones
on half-cleared slums or bomb-sites left unbuilt.
Then out of nowhere after years of silence
the words we used, our unobstructed accents,
will well up from the dark of childhood,
and once more on our lips we'll taste Greek salt.

[7]

I'd rather have been something scoured and gnarled
– bitten back to the bone as the pebbles
your waves revolve and the salt air cribbles –
an unrelinquishable will, a cold shard
chipped out of time, dug in. But I was made
from other stuff – I'd fixed my gaze
on whatever is unfixed and hazy
in myself and others. Being so loathe to act
I felt inaction kept my hopes intact.
I wanted to ferret out the evil at
the world's root, the cog that through the least quirk
seizes up the whole world's fluent clockwork.
I spilt the content of each instant and observed
how everything was tilting on the verge

of a total landslide and dispersal.
I'd choose and travel down one road
only to sense the constant tug to take
a different route entirely. No doubt
what I needed was the type of mind that cuts
clean through doubt. Or other books to read
than your page after page of thundering.
But I don't regret the way things are
now when the spell and fever of your song
untie the knots within me and already
your tidal roar is answering the stars.

Jamie McKendrick

In the Void

The sun's mane caught
in the cane stakes of the vegetable plots –
on the shore, seeming to doze, the odd lifeboat.

The day yielded no sound
beneath the polished arch,
not even a pine cone's thud
or bud's detonation,
on the other side of the walls.

Silence swallowed everything.
Our boat hadn't stopped,
cut the sand like razor wire; a sign long hovering in the air
plummeted.

Now the earth was an overflowing rim,
weight melted in the glare,

the blaze that was the dark's foam,
the pit widening, too deep
for us and for anchors.
                                Until suddenly
something happened, the trench sealed
shut, everything and nothing was lost.
And I was awake to the sound
of your rediscovered lips –
the vein imprisoned
in crystal
which waits to be released.

Simon Carnell and Erica Segre

En Route to Vienna

The baroque convent, all meerschaum and biscuit,
shaded a glimpse
of slow-moving water and laid tables,
strewn here and there with leaves
and lumps of ginger.

A swimmer emerged, shook himself
under a gnat-cloud,
inquired of our journey,
spoke at length of his own, over the border.

He pointed to the near bridge
which can be crossed (so he told us)
for a penny. He waved, dived,
was the stream itself . . .

                                And in his stead –
blazing the way for us – a little dachshund

bounded out of a garage, barking with joy,
one brotherly voice in the sultry haze.

Eamon Grennan

from Motets

The gondola that glides
in a harsh tar-and-poppy glare,
the deceiving song that rose
from piles of rope, the high doors
shut on you, and merriment
of masks disappearing in droves –

one evening in a thousand, and my night
is deeper! Down below
a blurred knot writhes arousing me
by fits and starts and makes me kin
to the intent eel-fisher on the shore.

*

The spirit that dispenses
forlana and rigadoon at each new
season of the street
feeds on secret passion, finds it
more intense at every turn.

Your voice is this irradiated essence.
By wire, by wing, by wind or chance,
favored by muse or instrument, it echoes,
happy or sad. I speak of something else
to one who doesn't know you, but its theme
is there insisting, *do re la sol sol* . . .

*

The hope of even seeing you again
was leaving me;

and I asked myself if this which closes off
all sense of you from me, this screen of images,
is marked by death, or if, out of the past,
but deformed and diminished, it entails
some flash *of yours*:

(under the arcades, at Modena,
a servant in gold braid dragged
two jackals on a leash).

Jonathan Galassi

The Coastguard House

A death-cell? The shack of the coastguards
is a box over the drop to the breakers;
it waits for you without an owner,
ever since the mob of your thoughts
bullied a welcome,
and stayed on there, unrequited.
You didn't take it to heart.

For years the sirocco gunned the dead stucco with sand;
the sound of your laugh is a jagged coughing;
the compass, a pin-head, spins at random;
the dizzy dice screw up the odds.
You haven't taken my possession to heart;
another time has thinned your nostalgia;
a thread peels from the spool.

I hold an end of it,
but the house balks backward;

its sea-green weathercock
creaks and caws without pity.
I keep one end of the thread,
but you house alone
and hold your hollow breath there in the dark.

Oh the derelict horizon,
sunless except for the
orange hull of a lonely, drudging tanker!
The breakers bubble on the dead-drop.
You haven't taken my one night's possession to heart;
I have no way of knowing
who forces an entrance.

Robert Lowell

Eastbourne

A brass band pumps out
something patriotic
from the pavilion on stilts,
which strides through the tide, as it rises,
erasing waterlogged hoofprints
from the sand along the shore.

A cold wind buffets me,
but the windows are touched by fire,
and the white mica of the cliff-faces
glitters from it in turn.

Bank Holiday. It brings back
the long wave of my own life
that has shuffled on its slope far too lethargically.
It's getting late. The great breakers
smash, then fritter away.

Now here come the war-wounded in their wheelchairs,
accompanied by long-eared dogs,
or taciturn children, or old folk.
(By tomorrow, no doubt, the whole thing
will look like a dream)

And here you come, too, untainted voice,
released from captivity and bewildered,
voice of my blood, lost to me
and restored late in the day.

As a hotel door revolves,
flashing a panel and another
picks it up and semaphores back
so I am caught up in the whirligig
that drags everything round. Just by listening
('my country!'), I can hear you breathing
and I get to my feet. The day's too much.

It will all come to seem futile, even
the force that seizes in one almighty clutch
living and dead, trees and rocks,
and that issues from you and through you. The fun
spares no one. There's more
blaring from the band. With dusk,
an ineffectual goodness seeps everywhere.

Evil triumphs. The wheel won't stop.

What's more, you knew it, Light in Darkness.

On this scorched spot,
from which you disappeared
at the first clang of bells,
all that remains is the quenched and acrid taper

which by now was
Bank Holiday.

Christopher Reid

The Storm

Les princes n'ont point d'yeux pour voir ces grand's merveilles,
Leurs mains ne servent plus qu'à nous persécuter . . .

Agrippa D'Aubigné, 'A Dieu'

The hard leaves on the magnolia
they're ruffled by thunder
then thumped by hailstones

(crystal and archaic the sounds
that chink in your nocturnal cabinet
and that grain of sugar
– a tiny lump of sleep yolk
stuck in your eyelid's shell
is all that's left of the gilt
inlay on mahogany
on badly scuffed leather bindings)

then the lightning makes trees and walls
famous for a moment
– marble a grain of manna
discandied I mean destroyed
– oh it's carved inside you
sister that sermon
you preach against me
it ties us closer than love can
– now the rude crash quiver
of timbrels (tumbrils I nearly said)

over the black ditch
then the fandango's yukky clatter
and some gesture that gropes or teases
– a little trailing capillary

                              as you turned you pushed

your smoky hair with one hand
and waved roughly with the other
                         then the darkness pitched on you

Tom Paulin

From the Train

With their neckbands of crimson, the turtledoves
have come to Sesto Calende for the first time
in living memory. That's
what the papers say. Leaning out the train window,
I looked for them in vain. A necklace of yours,
it's true, but in a different shade, made a reed-stem
bend at the top, then spilled its beads. It flashed
for my eyes only, falling into a pond. And
its flight of fire
blinded me to the other.

Eamon Grennan

The Eel

The self-same, the siren
of icy waters, shrugging off as she does the Baltic
to hang out in our seas,
our inlets, the rivers

through which she climbs, bed-hugger, who keeps going against
the flow, from branch to branch, then
from capillary to snagged capillary,
further and further in, deeper and deeper into the heart
of the rock, straining
through mud-runnels, till one day
a flash of light from the chestnut trees
sends a fizzle through a standing well,
through a drain that goes
by dips and darts from the Apennines to the Romagna –
that self-same eel, a firebrand now, a scourge,
the arrow-shaft of Love on earth
which only the gulches or dried-out
gullies of the Pyrenees might fetch and ferry back
to some green and pleasant spawning-ground,
a green soul scouting and scanning
for life where only
drought and desolation have hitherto clamped down,
the spark announcing
that all sets forth when all that's set forth
is a charred thing, a buried stump,
this short-lived rainbow, its twin met
in what's set there between your eyelashes,
you who keep glowing as you do, undiminished, among the sons
of man, faces glistening with your slime, can't you take in
her being your next-of-kin?

Paul Muldoon

from Xenia I

Dear little insect
whom we called Mosca – I don't know why –,
this evening just before dark
while I was reading Deutero-Isaiah
you reappeared at my side,
but not having your glasses
you couldn't see me,
and without their glinting
I couldn't be sure
it was you in the dusk.

2

Without glasses or antennae,
a poor insect who had wings
only in imagination,
a Bible coming unbound
and largely unreliable,
the black of night, a lightning flash,
a thunderclap, and then
no storm. Can it be
you were gone so quickly
without saying a word?
But it's ridiculous to think
you still had lips.

4

For the afterlife we had devised
a whistle, a sign of recognition.

I'm trying variations of it in the hope
we're all already dead without knowing it.

5

I've never understood
whether I was your dog,
faithful and sick with distemper,
or you were mine.
To others you were a myopic insect
at a loss in the blah-blah
of high society. They were naive,
those clever ones. They didn't know
they were your laughingstock:
that even in the dark you made them out
unmasking them
with that infallible sense of yours,
your bat-radar.

Harry Thomas

from Xenia II

5

I've descended, your arm in mine, almost a million stairs
and now that you're not here a void opens at every step.
Even so, our long journey was brief.
Mine still goes on, though I no longer feel the need
for connections, reservations,
mix-ups, the scorn of those who believe
that reality is what one sees.

I've descended millions of stairs, your arm in mine,
not, of course, because four eyes see better than two.

[53]

I descended them with you because I knew
that between us the only true pupils,
however clouded over, were yours.

Harry Thomas

In the Smoke

How many times I waited for you at the station
in the cold, the fog. I'd stroll up and down,
coughing, buying unspeakable newspapers,
smoking the Giubas later banned by that fool
the Minister of Tobacco.
Sometimes the wrong train, or one added late
or out of service. I'd inspect
the baggage carts, certain that I'd see
your bags and, behind them, you.
Then finally you appeared. It's a memory
among so many others, and it haunts my dreams.

Harry Thomas

Late at Night

A colloquy with the shades
isn't something for the telephone.
Our mute conversations are carried on
without a portable or loudspeaker.
And yet we attend to words
even when they don't concern us –
picked up by mistake by an operator
and connected to someone

who isn't there,
who doesn't hear.
One time they came from Vancouver
late at night
while I was holding for Milan. I was surprised
at first, then hoped the strange mistake
would go on. One voice from the Pacific,
the other from the lagoon. And that time
the two voices spoke freely as never before.
For a while nothing happened.
We assured the operator that everything
was all right, perfect, and so could –
in fact, *must* – continue. We never knew
who paid the bill for that miracle.
And I don't recall a word of it.
The time zone was different, the other
voice wasn't here, I wasn't there for her,
even the languages were jumbled, a pot-
pourri of jargon, swearing, and laughter.
Now after so many years the other voice
doesn't remember it and maybe believes I'm dead.
I believe she is the dead one.
For a time anyway she was alive
and was never aware of it.

Harry Thomas

My Muse

My Muse is distant; one could say
(this being the view of many) non-existent.
If ever there was one, she was got up like a scarecrow,
scarcely erect among the checkered vines.

[55]

She mills her arms as best she can, somehow still
upright, though a shade hunched, despite monsoons.
Even if the wind drops she can still move
as though to tell me Don't be afraid. Keep going.
As long as I can see you I'll give you life.

Some time ago my Muse deserted her lumber-room
of theatre costumes – whoever was dressed by her
cut a classy figure. Once I clothed myself
in her and she went off made up. But now she's got
just one sleeve left with which to conduct her quartet
of straw pipes. It's the only music I can stand.

Jamie McKendrick

Two Venetian Pieces

I

From the windows I could see typists.
Below, the alley, stink of fried shrimp,
some sickening stench from the canal.
A fine thing – Venice –
when she'd come such a long way,
to be looking out on a scene like this. She
who loved only Gesualdo, Bach, and Mozart, and I
the awful repertoire of opera, with a certain preference
for the worst. Then, to complicate things,
the clock which says five when it's four, dashing out
like a whirlwind – St Mark's, no one in Florian's,
Riva degli Schiavoni, Paganelli's Trattoria
(recommended by a tightfisted Tuscan painter),
two rooms not even adjoining, and the next day
seeing you breeze away, not even glancing

at my Ranzoni. I asked myself who was there
in your distraction – she, me, both of us? –
but following tracks that didn't run parallel,
travelling in fact in opposite directions.
And to think we'd concocted fantastic dreams
on those stone ramps
that lead from the far side of the Arno
to the great square. But now, there we were
among the pigeons, the strolling photographers,
the savage heat, the unread catalogue of the Biennale
weighing me down, difficult to get rid of.
We go back by boat – slipping on birdseed, buying
keepsakes postcards sunglasses from the stalls.
It was, I'd say, '34, and we too young or too odd
for a city which wants tourists only, and old lovers.

II

Just following orders, the talkative doorman –
grinning like one of Dante's devils –
said it was forbidden to disturb
the man of bullfights and safaris.
I beg him to try, I'm a friend of Pound's
(I exaggerated a little) and so deserve
some special treatment. Who knows. . . .
He picks up the receiver, talks, listens,
gabbles some more and – who'd believe it! –
Hemingway the bear has swallowed the hook.
He's still in bed. Only his eyes appear
and his spots of eczema, peering out
from underneath the fur blanket. Two
or three empty bottles of Merlot –
outriders of the great troop to follow.

Down in the restaurant everyone's eating.
We don't talk about him but our dear friend
Adrienne Monnier, Rue de l'Odeon,
Sylvia Beach, Larbaud, the roaring 'twenties,
the braying 'fifties. Paris a pigsty, ditto London,
New York *stinking*, plague-ridden. Nothing
to hunt in the marshes. No wild duck, no girls,
not even the idea for another book *like that*.
We draw up a list of common friends
whose names I pay no heed to. Everything
is *rotten*, rotten. Almost in tears,
 he insists I send him no more visitors
 like myself – all the worse if intelligent. Then
 he gets up, bundles himself in his bathrobe,
 and bids me *adieu* at the door with a hug. He lived
 two years after that and, dying twice,
 had time to read his own obituaries.

Eamon Grennan

SALVATORE QUASIMODO

[*1901–1968; b. Modica, Ragusa*]

Deadwater

Closed water, sleep of the marshes
broad-streaked, soaking poison,
now white, now green in lightning flashes,
you are like my heart.

Around, the grey of poplar and ilex,
leaves and acorns still within,
each with its uni-centred circles
frayed by the dark southwester drone.

So as on water memory
spreads its widening rings, my heart
moves from one point out and dies,
sister to you, deadwater.

Jack Bevan

And Suddenly It's Evening

Each of us is alone on the heart of the earth
pierced by a ray of sun:
and suddenly it's evening.

Jack Bevan

Elegy

Night's glacial messenger,
you return untarnished to the balconies

of ruined houses, illuminate
nameless tombs, derelict remains

of the smoking earth. Of our dream
this is what's left. And alone you head back
north, where everything hastens lightlessly
toward death, you the glimmering exception . . .

Martin Bennett

How Long the Night

How long the night, the moon pink and green
to the sound of your call among orange blossoms
when sharp with the dew you knock at a door
like a lord of creation: 'Let me in, let me in, beloved.'
The wind wrings snatches of hymns and laments
from the Iblei and Madonie peaks
on the timbrels of caves old as the aloe
and the eye of the brigand. And the Bear
stays with you still and shakes the seven
alarm fires lit on the hills,
and the rumble of the red carts of Saracens and Crusaders
stays with you still:
it may be the solitude, the converse, too,
with the starred creatures, the horse,
the dog, the frog; and the delirious
strumming of cicadas in the night.

Jack Bevan

On the Branches of Willows

And how could we have sung our own songs
with foreign heels upon our hearts,
amid the dead dumped in the squares
on the ice-stiffened grass: and the lamb-cry
of children, and the black scream
of the mother who came across her son
crucified on a telegraph pole?
On the branches of willows
our harps hung too in sacrifice,
turning lightly in the grey wind.

Bernard O'Donoghue

In a Remote City

It didn't appear from the sky,
but on the pale algae lawn of a northern garden:
a crow, leapt down from steep cover,
no symbol in the summer bent double
with rain and with rainbows –
but a crow as actual as an acrobat
on the Tivoli trapeze.
Brief apt figure that entered
the day that was ending in us
with its carousels water-wheels sea-shanties,
and the foghorn of a departing ship
spreading wings of churned foam
and the tears of the port's women.
The eager hour tolled
on this brink of Europe.

Still the crow was auspicious –
like others I'd figured
in a remote corner of the mind,
imagining an utterance that could shiver
the stalled world . . .
Unexpected power of a raised voice,
or a stake in violence? For a little irony's sake
all is lost – shed light more feared
than shade.
        Were you waiting on a new word
or on mine? The crow turned tail,
detached its quick feet from the lawn –
and vanished in the green air of your eye.

For a little irony's sake, all is lost.

Simon Carnell and Erica Segre

Footfall

And here is the sea and the flowering agave,
and the bright river parallel to ancient tombs
fitted into the wall like cells in a hive;
within mirrors, still smiling,
girls with their jet hair down.
One was at your side on an Ionian shore
(a bee shining sleeked with honey in her eye)
leaving barely a trace of her name,
in the shadow of the olive trees.
No-one to your rescue,
you know that a day like any other
plays across your face: a quick play of light
around the circle which encloses us –

on the other side of the moon
your soundless footfall,
crossing the threshold of Hades.

Simon Carnell and Erica Segre

The Soldiers Cry at Night

Neither the Cross nor childhood nor
Golgotha's hammer nor the memory
of an angel is enough to tear out
war. The soldiers cry
at night before dying, they are strong,
they fall at the feet of words
learned under the arms of life.
Love numbers the soldiers,
the nameless bursts of crying.

Edwin Morgan

Man of My Time

You are still the one with stone and sling,
man of my time. You were in the cockpit there
with your vicious wings, with the sundials of death.
I have seen you in the carts of fire, at the scaffold
and the wheels of torture. I have seen you, it was you,
with your neat sciences persuaded to extermination,
without love, without Christ. You've killed again,
as always, as the fathers killed, as the animals
killed when first they saw you.
This blood smells like the day
when the brother said to the other brother

[63]

'Let us go into the fields'. And that echo, cold, tenacious,
has reached right down to you in your own day.
Forget, sons, the clouds of blood
risen from the earth, forget the fathers:
their tombs are going down in ashes, black birds and the
  wind
are covering their hearts.

  Geoff Page and Loredana Nardi-Ford

SANDRO PENNA
[*1906–1977; b. Perugia*]

Country Cemetery

Amid the delight of crickets
dim brands' fire.

With on high the stars.

And an untried heart
at riotous rest
after splendid feats
and deeds of the day.

Yet even now a care clouds
the laughing eye
of the boy who followed
delight and me.

Blake Robinson

'Homeward bound. A freshet of blood'

Homeward bound. A freshet of blood
was laughing in the dust on my face.

This time, I'm not going home. Trampled
in the dust are my soul and my smile.

Blake Robinson

'It was in the movie house, the spot'

It was in the movie house, the spot
where two doors open and close all the time.
That clacking had her think
that he was to come back,
but he didn't.

Blake Robinson

'Graveyard lights, don't tell me'

Graveyard lights, don't tell me
the summer evening's not fine.
And fine the drinkers
in faraway inns.

Like antique friezes
they move under the sky
new with stars.

Graveyard lights, calm fingers
go counting slow evenings. Don't tell me
the summer night's not fine.

Blake Robinson

'How difficult, you know'

How difficult, you know,
loving you is and not loving
what art, which is serene
up on its altar, tells me.

Your earthly moods erase
with just a finger everything
numbing and chilling left
by myth about the forum.

Blake Robinson

For Eugenio Montale

Sundays toward twilight I go
the other way from the crowd,
that leaves the stadium. I don't look
at anyone, looking at all.
I may take in a smile, or rarely,
a holiday cry of greeting.

And I can't recall who I am.
Then I think it's too bad to die.
To die's so unfair, although
I don't recall who I am.

Blake Robinson

'We set out for summer's'

We set out for summer's
sculpted land.
Life was enough
for our love of life.

. . . A cop on the chalky road
was also a sensual treat.

Blake Robinson

'I have come down from the burning hill'

I have come down from the burning hill
to stand by the station's fresh urinal.
The dust and sweat that coat my skin
intoxicate me. In my eyes the sun
still sings. Body and soul I now abandon
to the lucid whiteness of the porcelain.

Jamie McKendrick

CESARE PAVESE

[*1908–1950; b. S. Stefano Belbo, Cuneo*]

Tolerance

It rains without sound into the meadow of the sea,
and no one passes in the filthy streets.
A woman got down off the train alone –
a vivid skirt under the raincoat, and the flash
of legs vanishing into the blackened doorway.

This place is like a land submerged. Evening
distils cold at every threshhold, and the houses
leak a bluish smoke in shadow. Red
windows are lighted. And a light comes on
between half-open shutters in the blackened house.

Next morning's cold, with sun on the sea.
A woman in her slip rinses her mouth out
at the fountain, and the spat foam's like rose wine.
Her hair's a dark-roots blonde, brittle as the orange-
peel
strewn on the ground. Stretching to the fountain
she can't outstare the filth-encrusted urchin, who's
enthralled.
Black-clad women push shutters open to the square,
their men still drowsing in the dark.

When night comes back the rain begins again,
sputtering in fires. Wives fan the coals to life,
one eye still on the blackened house
and the deserted fountain. The house
is blind with shutters, but there's a bed inside,
and on the bed a blonde's earning her living.

At night everything in this place closes –
everything except the blonde who washes in the
      morning.

Duncan Bush

The Paper Smokers

He took me to hear his band. He sat in a corner
and put the clarinet to his lips. Infernal uproar began.
Outside, a furious wind, thunder, rain and,
every five minutes or so, the lights dimming
between lightning-flashes. In the dark, faces
somehow convulsed from within – busking an old
      dance-tune
from memory. Demented, my poor friend
holds them together in the background. Then the clarinet
      writhes,
breaks through the brazen din, outstrips it, spends itself
like a single soul in a parched silence.

These cheap brass instruments are battered with dints:
these are peasants' hands holding the stops,
and the dogged foreheads hardly look up from the ground –
wretched, exhausted blood, worn out
by brutal work, you can hear it bellowing
through each note. And my friend laboriously leads them,
his own hands had hardened from hefting hammers,
pushing planes, wringing a living out of life.

Once he had comrades, and he's only thirty now.
He's one of the post-war generation, who grew up with
      hunger.
He came to Turin with all the rest, to find a living,

and he found injustice. He learnt to work
unsmiling, in the factories. To measure
the hunger of others against his own fatigue.
And he found injustice everywhere. He tried to find peace
in somnambulance along unending streets
at night, but all he saw was streets made desolate with
    light,
iniquity: raucous women, drunks,
lost, lurching puppets. He arrived in Turin
in winter, in the glare of factories, the filth of smoke.
And he discovered what work was. He accepted work
as the hard destiny of man – but only if all men
accepted it would there be justice in the world.
But he made comrades. He put up with endless talk
and had to listen, patiently, for it to end –
if he could just make comrades of them . . . Every house
    had
families of them. The city was ringed with them.
And the face of the world covered with them. They felt
in themselves enough desperation to conquer that
    world . . .

They sound rough tonight, the band, though
he's taught them one by one. He doesn't notice the
    drumming
rain, the lights dimming in unison. His face is fixed and
    grim,
like one anticipating grief, while he lips his clarinet.
I saw the same look in his eyes one night we were alone
with his brother, who's ten years sadder than he is,
trying to stay awake beside a falling light. His brother was
learning on a useless lathe he'd constructed himself.
And my poor friend accused destiny

of keeping him in debt to his plane and his hammer,
just to feed two old people no one wanted.

                                    Suddenly he shouted
that it wasn't destiny if the world suffered,
    if the light of the sun wrung a curse from you:
    it was men who were to blame. *At least we could get out,*
        be free to choose hunger, and say no
        to a life that makes use of love and pity
        the family, the little plot of earth, to tie our hands.

Duncan Bush

The Country Whore

The front wall of the yard
often reflects the first sunlight,
like the cow-shed used to. And at morning, when her body
    rouses
in the untidied room, there's no one with her,
only the smell of those first clumsinesses.
Even the body tangled in the sheets is the same one
it always was, when the heart bounded with discovery.

She wakes alone and late to morning's call
and out of the grievous half-light up there swims up
the abandonment of another wakening: the cow-shed
of her childhood, and the blazing lassitude of sunlight
at somnolent doorways. A faint, familiar scent
loaded with the musk of sweat-soaked
hair, and the livestock snuffing at it. Her body
takes a furtive pleasure in the sun's
insinuations, suffusing her like a caress.

Getting out of bed eases her legs –
they're youthful, thickset, still a girl's.
The awkward little girl who inhaled the odours
of tobacco and hay, and quivered to the man's
brief touch: she liked to play.
Sometimes she and the man played that game lying down,
but he didn't sniff at her hair:
the haggling over, he was rummaging her in the hay.
His weight squashing down on her was like her father's.
The scent, flowers pestled on stone.
It comes back often in slow wakenings,
that far-off smell of flowers bruised to juice,
and of the cow-shed, and sun. A man wouldn't know
the subtle caress of that bitter memory.
A man wouldn't see, beyond the body lying there,
that spilt childhood's awkward longing.

Duncan Bush

Dina Thinking

It's a joy to jump in this water, now flowing so clear
and fresh in the sun: nobody's here at this hour.
The husks of the poplars startle me more, when they touch
me,
than the slap of the water as I plunge in. It's still dark under
there,
and the cold is killing, but as soon as you jump back out
into the sunlight, you see the world with washed eyes.

It's a joy to lie naked in grass that's already warm
and to gaze up with half-closed eyes at the high hills
that rise over the poplars and look down on me naked

and nobody up there can tell. That old man in his hat
and his underwear, fishing one day, saw me dive in,
but thought I was a boy and never uttered a word.

This evening I'll return as a woman in a red dress –
those men who smile at me out on the street don't know
I'm lying here naked right now – I'll go back dressed
to gather their smiles. Those men don't know it
but tonight in my red dress my hips will be stronger
and I'll be a new woman. Nobody sees me down here:
and beyond these bushes are sand-diggers stronger
than those men who smile: but nobody sees me.
Men are so silly – tonight as I dance with them all
it'll be as if I was naked, like now, and no one will know
they could've found me right here. I'll be just like them.
Except that those fools will want to pull me too close
and whisper proposals like con men. But what do I care
for the caresses of men? I can touch me all by myself.
But I wish we could be naked in front of each other tonight
without smiling like con men. I smile to myself now,
and stretch out in the tall grass, and nobody knows.

Geoffrey Brock

Two Cigarettes

Each night's a liberation. You see light reflecting
on the asphalt avenues that open wide to the wind.
Each of the few passersby has a face and a story.
But nobody's tired at this time of night: thousands of
    streetlamps
just for people who pause to rummage for matches.

The small flame dies on the face of the woman

who's asked for a match. It dies in the wind,
and so, disappointed, she asks for another.
It too goes out, and now she laughs softly.
We could speak loud here, we could shout:
no one would hear. We turn our gaze
toward all the dark windows – eyes closed in sleep –
and we wait. The woman hunches her shoulders
and laments that she lost her colorful scarf,
as good as a heater at night. But leaning together
against a corner reduces the wind to a breath.
Already one cigarette butt lies on the worn asphalt.
The scarf was from Rio, she tells me, but now
she's glad to have lost it, because she's met me.
If the scarf came from Rio, it must have spent nights
on an ocean flooded with light by a great liner –
windy nights, certainly. It was a gift from a sailor;
one who's no longer around. She whispers to me
that, if I'd like to come up, she'll show me his picture –
curly-haired, bronzed. He worked on a dirty steamer,
cleaning the engines. She says I'm better-looking.

Two butts, now, on the asphalt. We look at the sky:
that window up there, she says pointing, is ours –
but the heater's not working. At night, lost steamers
have little to steer by, maybe only the stars.
We cross the street, arm in arm, playfully warming each
    other.

Geoffrey Brock

'Death will come and will have your eyes'

Death will come and will have your eyes –
this death that accompanies us
from morning till evening, unsleeping,
deaf, like an old remorse
or an absurd vice. Your eyes
will be a useless word,
a suppressed cry, a silence.
That's what you see each morning
when alone with yourself you lean
toward the mirror. O precious hope,
that day we too will know
that you are life and you are nothingness.

Death has a look for everyone.
Death will come and will have your eyes.
It will be like renouncing a vice,
like seeing a dead face
reappear in the mirror,
like listening to a lip that's shut.
We'll go down into the maelstrom mute.

Geoffrey Brock

LEONARDO SINISGALLI
[*1908–1981; b. Montemurro, Potenza*]

Dog Flies

Fido has fat buttocks.
He's an old church dog
who loafs under the altar.
He's lost his sense of smell, his fangs
are loose and he's given up
scratching himself with his muzzle.
Even cats scare him
but he's here at the requiem mass
for my mother's bones.
His head stretched out between his paws,
he's stuck out his tongue: suddenly
he swallows a big fly that was bothering him.

Jamie McKendrick

My Mother

My mother had a strange way of stroking my face: she
would press her palm against my snout, almost crush-
ing my lips and pull me suddenly backwards to kiss the
nape of my neck. I closed my eyes in a swoon I thought
would turn to sleep. But she regretted it – she wanted
me strong and would push me away so I ended standing
with my feet on the ground where black carob seeds lay
scattered.

Jamie McKendrick

The Canaries

The day Pope Pacelli* died
Mother Pasqualina Lehnert
barely had time
to bundle her stuff together
before taking her leave
of the papal palaces.
She filled two bags and carried off
the cage with the two canaries –
Gretel and Dompfaff.

Jamie McKendrick

* Maria Giuseppe Eugenio Pacelli, Pope Pius XII from 1938 to 1958. Since his death he has been criticised, and defended, for his neutrality towards the Third Reich, and has had the title 'Venerable' (a step towards beatification and sainthood) conferred upon him by Pope John Paul II. [Translator's note]

ALFONSO GATTO
[1909–1976; b. Salerno]

They Could Call You Dead

Your eyes are, like youth, big and lost,
and they depart from the world.
One could say you were quietly dead
and roll the sky on you, step by step,
in pursuit of the dawn.
You are the love one carries in one's arms
while running towards the sea, towards the wind:
To say you are something cold to be warmed by the fire,
something sad with dark hair
to be eternally combed, is like
consigning you to silence, or standing by you
while the water is beating on the shore.

G. Singh

Anniversary

I remember those days:
in the unpredictable morning it was the fear
of being left alone that woke us up.
I heard the sky like a dead voice.
And the light abandoned by the dying
on the window-panes touched my forehead;
it left traces of its endless sleep
on my hair. No human cry was heard,
only snow. Each one behind that wall
was alive – alive merely to weep,
and silence absorbed the whole flood of human tears.

Oh, frozen to the very core,
Europe shall never warm up again; together with the dead
who love her eternally, she'll be lonely and white
without limits, made one by snow.

G. Singh

ATTILIO BERTOLUCCI

[*1911–2000*]

Wind

It is like a wolf, the wind
That descends from the hills onto the plain,
In the fields it lays flat the grain,
Wherever it goes leaving dismay behind.

It whistles when mornings are clear
Lighting up houses and skyline,
It dishevels the water in the fountain,
Chases men indoors to the fire.

Then, weary, it falls asleep and a stupor
Takes all things, as after making love.

Charles Tomlinson

October Night

Your solitary song awakened me,
sad friend of October, innocent owl.
It was night,
swarming with dreams like bees.

They kept up their buzzing
agitating fiery tresses
and blond beards,
but their eyes were red and sad.

You sang, melancholy
as an oriental captive

under her azure sky.
I could hear the beating of my heart.

Charles Tomlinson

The Years

The mornings of our lost years,
the tables in the sunny autumn shade,
the friends who went and then returned, the friends
who will never return again, I thought of them with joy.

Because this September day is shining
so beguilingly into windows of shops in hours
like those of then; those of then
are gliding by at a peaceful tempo now,

the crowd is the same on golden pavements,
only the grey and lilac
are changed by fashion into green and red,
the pace is slow and easy, that of the provinces.

Charles Tomlinson

The Ants

The ants on the full-grown trunk of the acacia
profit from the sun that warms October days,
minute by minute, up and down on the rough bark of the
        tree.

The ants are toiling against the coming winter:
if I shift my glance to the light of the highway here
it is men and women I see toiling up and down.

O single spirit of beings who live beside me
on this open plain bravely preparing to face the snow
help me confront the extinction of the daylight,

over our unequal houses the kindling night.

Charles Tomlinson

Portrait of a Sick Man

This man you see here, portrayed in red and black
and who occupies the entire spacious picture
is me at the age of forty-nine wrapped up
in an ample dressing-gown that cuts the hands half off

as if they were flowers; you cannot tell whether the body
is lying down or is on a chair: it is like this with the sick
placed before windows framing the light of day –
another day doled out to eyes soon weary.

But when I ask the artist, my son of fourteen years,
whose portrayal he intended, he at once declares:
'One of those Chinese poets you had me read
as he gazes upon the world – in one of his last hours.'

What he says is true – now I remember giving him that book
which restores the heart with its celestial shores
and dark autumnal leaves: in it sages, or poets feigning sage
graciously take leave of life, their glasses raised.

Only I, who belong to a century that believes
it tells no lies, recognise in that sick man
myself lying to myself: and I take up my pen
to exorcise a sickness I do and do not believe in.

Charles Tomlinson

Butterflies

Why do butterflies always go about in pairs
and if one gets lost in a thicket of Buddleia
the other doesn't saunter off but stays
and bats its wings in a baffled way as though
against a prison wall which is no other
than this gold of a day already darkening
at five o'clock with October almost here?

– You'd lost her, perhaps you thought, but there she is
airborne again, incorrigibly veering
towards a zone, that darkness has designs on,
of Sunday fields and vineyards, ploughed and picked:
and all you have to do is follow her
into the night, just as you waited in the jittery sunshine
till she'd drunk her fill of the juice of autumn flowers.

Jamie McKendrick

GIORGIO BASSANI

[*1912–2000; b. Ferrara*]

Salute to Rome

Goodbye limed sand, goodbye diamond,
your sky is a closed face above me,
let me return to my home town entombed
in grass as in a warm and high sea.

Burning gates in the distant sky,
your sun is black, it's black your moon.
Flesh without regret, laughter without one
memory: hopeless city, goodbye.

Since I know your streets, straight swords, the tones
of your celestial squares; but I know the gales
that hone you, the wails
from your hidden stations.

No, your brow doesn't shine with grace.
Who'll gather you, cry of jubilation?
The rainbow mirroring you is cloudless.
You're alone, within your walls of space.

Peter Robinson

Towards Ferrara

At this hour when through the hot endless grasses
the last trains make their way towards Ferrara,
their languid whistles fade as sleep engulfs them
along with the lingering red on village towers.

Mead from damp meadows enters the train windows
and takes the shine off bare wood benches. The fingers
of tired lovers unlace like ragged silk,
their parched lips now a desert without kisses.

Jamie McKendrick

GIORGIO CAPRONI
[1912–1990; b. Livorno]

For Her

For her, I want words that rhyme
plainly, in real time.
Rhymes that may not have been dared
before, but are open, well-aired.
Rhymes that partake
of the nautical jingle her earrings used to make.
Or that have picked up a note
of the coral she wore at her throat.
Rhymes that even from a distance
(Annie always spoke her mind)
transmit an elegance
both scant and refined.
Rhymes that won't just disappear,
having tickled the ear.
Rhymes, not of the fading light,
but green, full of fight.

Christopher Reid

'Ottone's its name'

Ottone's its name
– next after Gorreto, to the north
of Liguria: the first
large Emilian town.

Once a village of cattle
with a sizeable market. Of all

that antique opulence today
only the vast square remains –
its three hotels, the green light
through the horsechestnuts and sheer
above the Trebbia the mill
still beating and treading
water with its wheel.

And it's there
in that wooded hollow,
where the occasional
pheasant breaks cover,
that I should like to call it a day.
There where life stagnates
(or seems to) without
the motor force of time. Time
without the force of life.

Jamie McKendrick

After the News

The wind . . . There remained the wind.
A slack wind, bald earth, and the leaf
(of a newspaper) the wind
shifts up and down
on the asphalt's grey. The wind
and nothing else. Not even
no one's dog who at vespers
slips, even him, in church
to seek a master. Not even,
on that switchback road
high above the gravel path, the fool

who every time runs
to meet the local bus, to await
– as he said – himself, gone away
to purchase discernment. The wind
and grey of the shutters
pulled down. The grey
of the wind on the asphalt. And nothingness.
The nothingness of *that* leaf
in the illiterate wind. A wind
slack and distracted – a breath
without spirit, quite dead.
Nothing else. Not even the dejection.
The wind and nothing else. A wind
without people. *That* wind,
there where Augustinianly
time no longer happens.

Peter Robinson

VITTORIO SERENI

[*1913–1983; b. Luino*]

from Algerian Diary
to Remo Valianti

I

Over there where from tower
to tower agreement
leaps in vain now and is thrown back,
the who-goes-there of the hour,
– just as down here from turret to turret
from the heights of the compound
Moroccan guards call to each other –
who goes in the gloomy midnight's
quick snowflakes, who misses
the final toast on the wind's
black thresholds, sinister
with waiting, who goes . . .
It's an image of ours
distorted, not come
to light, which abandons
a blue vein of oblivion only
between two eras dead in us.

Sainte-Barbe du Thélat, New Year's Day 1944

Peter Robinson and Marcus Perryman

6

They don't know they're dead
the dead like us,

they have no peace.
Stubbornly they repeat life,
speak words of goodness to each other,
reread the age-old signs in the sky.
A grey circle runs in Algeria
through the months' derision
but the axis is fixed to a scorched name: ORAN

Saint-Cloud, August 1944

Peter Robinson and Marcus Perryman

9

He's flying high now
– he's out of it – on wings –
the first soldier to hit
which beach in Normandy?
and fall flat
I know it because someone touched
me on the shoulder and whispered
ever so gently
pray for Europe our Europe
just as that steel Armada
was bunching up to the coast of France

halfasleep I replied
it's the wind's frappy sound
only that
but if really and truly
you were the first to fall down
on that beach
– was it Arromanches? –
try if you can

to say a prayer
for I'm dead
both to the war and the peace
– the music I hear
is a flapflack as the guy-ropes
they beat against the tentpoles
and the stretched canvas
– it's not the music of angels in heaven
but for me
under this red canvas cross
it's all the music I'll get
– like a crutch or a grudge
long years in the nursing
it's my basic
my only ration

Hospital Camp 127, June 1944

Tom Paulin

A Dream

I was crossing the bridge
over a river that could have been the Magra
where I go for the summer, or even the Tresa,
in my part of the country between Germignaga and Luino.
A leaden body without face blocked my way.
'Papers,' he ordered. 'What papers,' I answered.
'Out with them,' he insisted, firm,
on seeing me look aghast. I made to appease him:
'I've prospects, a place awaiting me,
certain memories, friends still alive,
a few dead honourably buried.'

'Fairy tales,' he said, 'you can't pass
without a programme.' And sneering he weighed up
the few papers, my worldly goods.
I wanted one last try. 'I'll pay
on my way back if you'll let me
pass, if you'll let me work.'
We would never see eye to eye: 'Have you made,'
he was snarling, 'your ideological choice?'
Grappling we struggled on the bridge's parapet
in utter solitude. The fight
still goes on, to my dishonour.
I don't know
who'll end up in the river.

Peter Robinson and Marcus Perryman

Saba

Beret pipe stick, the lifeless
objects of a memory.
But I saw them brought to life on one
roaming in an Italy of dust and rubble.
Always he talked of himself
but like no one I've known who talking of themselves
and demanding life of others in his talk
gave as much and so much more
to anyone who'd stay and listen.
And one day, a day or two after the 18th of April,
I saw him wandering from square to square
from one Milan café to another
hounded by the radio.
'Bitch' – he was railing – 'bitch.' In amazement
people looked at him.

It was Italy he meant. Abrupt, as to a woman
who knowingly or not has wounded us to death.

Peter Robinson and Marcus Perryman

MARIO LUZI
[b. 1914, Castello, Florence]

Night Cleans the Mind

Night cleans the mind.

A little later we are here as you well know,
a line of souls along the edge,
some ready to leap, others almost in chains.

Someone on the sea's page
traces a sign of life, fixes a point.
Occasionally a seagull appears.

Jamie McKendrick

Year

Providential now, and unprotesting
the wicker racks and urns are taken out.
Grapes hang. The other is unknown, the other
was and is closed in this opaque sky
where a wine-coloured light thickens
and the finch's cry already tells of frost.

It's here, and in these mild clear tasks
that what I don't possess yet still must lose
is spent and burnt away.
Time past and still to come cuts loose . . .
I have come here, a remnant
of inscrutable times – ardent, waiting.
Endlessly I become what I am,
find repose in this empty light.

Jamie McKendrick

FRANCO FORTINI
[1917–1944; b. Florence]

Letter

Father, day by day the world defeated you
  as I who am like you will also be defeated.

Father, your gestures are no more than air in air
  as my words are drowned like wind in the wind.

Father, they betrayed you and stripped you of your pride.
  No one cast a glance your way to help you.

Father of the narrow joy, of the burnt-up heart,
  Father, saddest of my brothers, father –

Your dear son still trembles at your trembling
  as on that childhood day of rain and fear

When pale at the twisted rabbi's wailings
  you let fall handfuls of earth on your own father's coffin.

But what you didn't speak I must speak for you
  at the throne of light which consumes my days.

For this your son has set off, and now with his companions
  seeks out the rough white roads of Gallilee.

Jamie McKendrick

The Animal

In the night some kind of animal
killed a tiny beast, below the house. On the tiles
which a fine sun brightens

it's left a bloody smear,
a small pile of violet guts
and gall-bladder all gold.
Who knows where it pleases itself, where sleeps, where
    dreams
of biting and taking in a flash
from its victim's stomach
the fetid, bitter parts.
I see the ocean, it's sky-blue, cheerful the sails.
And it's not true.
The little, bloodthirsty animal
has gnawed into the poison
and blind with light now
cries and fights and from the thorns begs mercy.

Marcus Perryman and Peter Robinson

Genre Theory

For twenty years, at a point on the stairs
which lead through plants from house to street
I've seen some winged insects in mid-air
resembling wasps or flies
but which are neither wasps nor flies,
tiny helicopters in the rapidest beat
of the wings almost hanging. I've asked myself why
if not always quite often they stop there and not elsewhere,
whether it be a sunbeam lights on them or shadow
already fallen there. And I think it's because
imperceptible currents
are rising, ridges
of temperature from stems, leaves, plants.

I was watching one of those insects once more
hover in mid-air; and at the same time read
almost as if I were humming a tune
the letter of a man who lives in the country
around Siena, where holding illusions is easier.
He thanked me for writing. It was
– he said – like 'a voice given
to one who travails alone upon the hills.'
The verb 'to travail', I recall, was one of my mother's.
Even that 'voice given', that 'upon the hills' has the ring
of centuries wrung dry. The pastoral
is in the wings' light humming, all
tragedy is far away.

Marcus Perryman and Peter Robinson

Reading a Poem*

I read lines by Sereni
for a friend who died years back, recall
that friend of his and the house he'd lived in.

And when Sereni had accompanied
his friend's body to the Verano cemetery
by the autostrada beyond the Appenines he returned
staring at five hundred kilometers one by one
little by little reflecting
towards this city
which in sunny mornings on the water-meadows wavers.

Others I've never understood nor myself,
but only the way I fail to. If a truth

* The poem by Sereni referred to here is 'Niccolò' in *Stella variabile* (1981).
[Translator's note]

hits me it's between the eyes: it is
an accusation. I reason
without understanding. Never am I where I believe.

That morning I must have spoken
like the idiot I know I am. Some bright saliva
I'll have had on my lips. Some sustenance
for my days as far as night.
With mistaken steps to reach as far as night.
Incredulous, Sereni looked at me
offended, no, but stupefied. He was
sitting at his desk and in his bloodshot eyes
the great constructions of his own death lived on.

Courtesy and grace I don't know well what they are.
Within the bus bearing us there's such an uproar
it permits neither speech
nor remaining silent humanly.
A wrong's been done me, I don't know when.
A strange indecipherable injustice
has rendered me for ever hard and foolish.
I read lines by Sereni for Niccolò Gallo
and once again write word by word.
Not everything's true then of what I've said so far.
I can, even I, understand who we are.

Marcus Perryman and Peter Robinson

The Hour of Vile Deeds

Everything is clear now,
the words in the books all
come true. All the others know it.
They told you to take two paces forward

in the middle of the yard of rain and wind
and its yellow lamps before the dawn.
You see the great mastiffs in leather aprons
unloading the sides of human meat
for the cold storage chambers, and sawdust
under the chromium hooks. The receipts
are stamped at the gate
where a van waits with open doors.
Then it was day and the postmen
shook their oilskins in the porter's lodges.

Paul Lawson

Translating Brecht

A huge thunderstorm
rolled around in coils all afternoon above
the roof-tops before it broke in flashes and sheeted down.
I stared at the lines of cement and glass
that walled up screams and wounds and limbs
including mine, which I have survived. Warily, looking
now up at the roof-tiles doing battle, now at the dry page,
I listened to the word
of a poet perish or change
into another voice we no longer hear. The oppressed
are oppressed and quiet, quietly the oppressors
talk on the phone, hatred is polite, and even I
believe I no longer know who is to blame.

Write, I tell myself, hate
those who sweetly lead into nothingness
the men and women who walk beside you
and believe they do not know. Write your name too

among those of the enemy. The storm
has passed away with all its bluster. Nature
is far too feeble to mimic battles. Poetry
changes nothing. Nothing is certain, but write.

Paul Lawson

PRIMO LEVI

[*1919–1987; b. Turin*]

Reveille

In the brutal nights we used to dream
Dense violent dreams,
Dreamed with soul and body:
To return; to eat; to tell the story.
Until the dawn command
Sounded brief, low:
    '*Wstawać*':
And the heart cracked in the breast.

Now we have found our homes again,
Our bellies are full,
We're through telling the story.
It's time. Soon we'll hear again
The strange command:
    '*Wstawać*'.

11 January 1946

Ruth Feldman and Brian Swann

For Adolf Eichmann

The wind runs free across our plains,
The live sea beats for ever at our beaches.
Man makes earth fertile, earth gives him flowers and fruits.
He lives in toil and joy; he hopes, fears, begets sweet
    offspring.

. . . And you have come, our precious enemy,
Forsaken creature, man ringed by death.

What can you say now, before our assembly?
Will you swear by a god? What god?
Will you leap happily into the grave?
Or will you at the end, like the industrious man
Whose life was too brief for his long art,
Lament your sorry work unfinished,
The thirteen million still alive?

Oh son of death, we do not wish you death.
May you live longer than anyone ever lived.
May you live sleepless five million nights,
And may you be visited each night by the suffering of
    everyone who saw,
Shutting behind him, the door that blocked the way back,
Saw it grow dark around him, the air fill with death.

20 July 1960

Ruth Feldman and Brian Swann

Shemà

You who live secure
In your warm houses,
Who return at evening to find
Hot food and friendly faces:

        Consider whether this is a man,
        Who labors in the mud
        Who knows no peace
        Who fights for a crust of bread
        Who dies at a yes or a no.
        Consider whether this is a woman,
        Without hair or name

With no more strength to remember
Eyes empty and womb cold
As a frog in winter.

Consider that this has been:
I commend these words to you.
Engrave them on your hearts
When you are in your house, when you walk on your way,
When you go to bed, when you rise.
Repeat them to your children.
Or may your house crumble,
Disease render you powerless,
Your offspring avert their faces from you.

10 January 1946

Ruth Feldman and Brian Swann

August

Who stays in the city in August?
Only the poor and the mad,
Forgotten little old ladies,
Pensioners with their little dogs,
Thieves, some gentlemen and the cats.
Through the deserted streets
You hear a continual tapping of heels,
See women with plastic bags
In the streak of shade along the walls.
Under the fountain with its small tower
In the pool green with algae
There's a middle-aged naiad
About four inches long
With nothing on but a brassière.

A few yards farther on,
Despite the well-known prohibition,
The begging pigeons
Surround you in a flock
And steal the bread out of your hand.
Rustling in the sky, in weary flight,
You hear the noontime demon.

22 July 1986

    Ruth Feldman and Brian Swann

NELO RISI
[b. 1920, Milan]

Italy

She's a woman with her heart in the south
but what she wears is rich stuff from the north.
Courted by businessmen, at the mercy of
canny, quick-fingered folk, she's lost
her smile and her lovely body's left
stained among tombstones.

But still they set her up in the pose
of the Madonna, girt in a sky-blue mantle
for the family photo. Gravid in armchairs,
governers and priests have fashioned
a crown for her.

               She's no longer a mother to us
– averse to offspring, she gives birth
to disasters. Over the incessant
hum of motors there's no mistaking
the hammer blows as they prepare
her long narrow coffin.

Jamie McKendrick

The TV News

Crouched in a ring of shadow
like savages round a fire
some image of extermination
good-naturedly enters the family circle.

Thus every evening we theorize
upon the violence of history.

Jamie McKendrick

ANDREA ZANZOTTO
[*b. 1921, Pieve di Soligo*]

Where Are They?*

Where on earth is the dearest of my aunts
who used to write little plays
in verse for Carnival and other holidays
with Latin words thrown in to boot;
many people still remember them.
'She started drinking,' they said,
to drown her sorrows.
Who knows. But only she knows
how much, in this scribbling, I resemble her.

*

Where is Pina who sold newspapers
and her little shop behind the square
with colors bright as street lights . . .
'Coal and newspapers for sale':
blacker than a chimney, with piles
of coal all around, and in the middle – what bells! what
   rattles!–
the red blue green of the newspapers
spread and grew
like a marvellous meadow–
though the coal came up to our eyelashes.

*

* Like 'For Eugenio Montale on His Eightieth Birthday', 'Where Are They?' is
written in a rural Veneto dialect. Some stanzas of 'Where Are They?' have
been omitted and the last stanza here included reverts to Italian in the
original.

Where – among my aunt's friends,
all so good and so strange –
is the widow Bres, who came from Belluno
and always had winning lottery numbers
and had inherited a stack of money too
(eighty thousand lire) from her husband
but then frittered it all away
having fun, going on sprees with her friends:
nothing but hearty soups, grappa, eggs,
glasses of wine and all the rest,
even if certain people don't believe it.

*

Where is Aurora and the cookies,
the dried carob beans, the crab apples that she sold
to children for a penny, what booming business
on holidays in the evenings the kids gave her!
On a camp stove, meanwhile, resting on the windowsill,
her supper would be boiling.
One time some big kids
put a small chunk of mulberry in her soup–
and when she tried it with her fork it seemed awfully hard –
'The world's going to hell in a handbasket,' she used to say.

[. . .]

Good and kindly souls
I don't know if I've done wrong
by reducing you to decals
or maybe to streaks and spiderwebs
on the windshield of an old car
that drags along in the stormy night,
good and saintly souls
of the quarter and also beyond

Ah, but a strange odor seems to be rising
from a corner of the courtyard,
an odor deep, dark, and sticky
that enfolds and dazes you
in its snare –
but precious beyond words –
it's the odor of silkworms
thousands of them on their trellises.

Tiny jaws that dribble,
coins that fall into the money-box . . .
And you, although you feel out of place, are almost content
and you are thinking of an insect, more ugly than beautiful,
one wrapped, however, in its silk
up there in the seventh heaven.

Ruth Feldman and John P. Welle

For Eugenio Montale on His Eightieth Birthday

You don't like to see coals carried to Newcastle,
(although that's what I'm doing)
owls brought to Athens or firewood and brambles to the
    forest.
That's why it seems so difficult, and bizarre too,
to send you a poem, Eusebius –
unless it were one of those sonnets cut, like chips of
    kindling, just right,
like the ones they used to draft by candlelight
bundled up in a heavy cloak against the cold in the great
    days gone by.
This time I risk making a mess of things
and I'm mixed up worse than usual;

how much better a deep silence, keeping quiet and reading
        your poems.
And yet, because of those rifle shots,
those mine explosions in the rarest void
of the countrysides, of the worlds,
and even more for that crackle of squibs
blown upward in festival flashes
in the vortices of wind
in the very heart of storm clouds, –
that always bud and bloom from your poetry, –
and always rouse me
and which, many years ago, showed me a road
as in the middle of a fog bank –
that's why I must greet you today.
I don't know if I have gone straight or if I have deviated,
if these lines, sent from distant cliffs and slopes,
merit understanding.
But I'm sure that you see how clear
is the wish that I (along with many others)
make for your eighty years of this human life,
and perhaps a thousand more as well of your jolting-
        entrancing us
with your darkness, your sparkle,
your hedgehog obscurity and self-disclosure:
branches and roots of the same forest
where the easy and the difficult tangled up together
are always themselves and always their opposites.

Ruth Feldman and John P. Welle

The Apotheosis of Snow

How many perfections are there, how many,
how many totalities? The data points stack up, and then
then it starts – abstraction, astrification, formulation of
    stars,
assideration and traversal of sidereal space,
assiderations, assimilations.
And I would proceed up through the perfected,
on further from the great dazzlement, from the plenum and
    the void,
procedures researched, procedures rehearsed,
both obvious and oblique,
both doubtful and shadowy (if I knew then I'd tell).
But what of sustenance would that give, so great the
    abundance of snow,
or value: to valley from morning to valley,
to mountain from the light's many fountains.
I set myself central to this radiant motion
or is that inanition – and ah!
And ah, the first shivers of leaping, of grasping,
they set out in line, so sure of themselves,
that's it, what more do you want?

Your consolation, your insolation,
acclimatized and allied
are what I get from this winter
on vitreous vertices of the eternal, on the frozen margins
of that which I-never-no-didn't-let go,
and the star that burns in its rind
and the chestnut drawn to the ice's kind
and all Eros all hero all lib-liberty in the snare

in whose bear-hug I find myself trammelled, found too
there is found in suggestion, stands in the programme, and
    the execution
a smile, *n'est-ce pas?* And exist (tense) (i.e.) (that is to see)
something that we can do nothing about, not even
    hypothesize
on the threshold where one makes to (caress?).
A bacchanal shout screes over the glacier
the culture of colours
the reassured workings in gold.
Hello. Who's calling? Hang up again.
And I'm ready too, in immortal disguise
for a thumbnail sketch of the snow
– a blip even on the radar would do –
Hello anyone there?
To or of the perfected.

'That's all then, you can go.'

Peter Rafferty

GIORGIO ORELLI

[*b. 1921, Airolo, Switzerland*]

In the Family Circle

A funerary light, one quenched,
refreezes the conifers
with their bark that endures beyond death,
and all is still in this shell
hollowed out tenderly by time:
in the family circle
from which it makes no sense to flee.

Within a silence so well-known
the dead are more alive than the living:
from cleaned rooms smelling of camphor
they come down by trap-doors in stoves
replenished with wood, adjust their own
    portraits,
revisit the stall to look once more
at the brown, pure-bred animals.

                      Yet,
without moling tools, without umbrellas
for ensnaring swallows;
not cautious, not unmindful in the chase,
behind what carillon do you head off,
boys across benumbed meadows?

The whetstone's in its horn.
The henhouse rests on its elder.
Daddy-long-legs stay a long while
entangled on the church walls.
The fountain accompanies itself with water.

And me, to a more
discreet love of life restored . . .

Peter Robinson

Rhine Eels

The eels that arrive here from the Rhine
don't die easily. Prodded
by the fishvender they writhe
blackly in the sparse ice
on the white polystyrene.
The gazer turned purchaser
asks for two. A woman weighs them
then suddenly cries out: 'It's escaped!'
With an assured dart, the smaller one
has leapt from the scales onto the porphyry
slabs of the square, but soon it's all over,
and the creature's grabbed hold of.
Cutting them into pieces isn't enough
to stop them living.

Jamie McKendrick

PIER PAOLO PASOLINI

[*1922–1975; b. Bologna*]

from Gramsci's Ashes
(*after Pasolini*)

There's nothing May-like in this toxic air
which further darkens or with blazing light
blinds the dark garden of the foreigner
and nothing May-like in the soapy cloud
casting its veil on the vast amphitheatre
of yellow attics ranged beside the mud
of the Tiber and among the purple pines
of Rome. Autumnal spring spreads mortal peace,
though disabused like all our destinies,
over the ancient stones, exhausted now,
and finished ruins where the strong
ingenuous impulse to start life anew
crumbled; and now silence, hot but hard,
where a motorbike whines off into the blue.
A boy in that far spring when even wrong
was at least vigorous, that Italian spring
our parents knew, vital with earth and song
and so much less distracted, when the place
united in fanaticism, you drew
already, brother, with your skinny paw
the ideal society which might come to birth
in silence, a society not for us
since we lie dead with you in the wet earth.
There remains now for you only a long
rest here in the 'non-Catholic' cemetery,
a last internment though this time among
boredom and privilege; and the only cries

you hear are a few final hammer-blows
from an industrial neighbourhood which rise
in the evening over wretched roofs, a grey
rubble of tin cans and scrap metal where
with a fierce song a boy rounds out his day
grinning, while the last rain falls everywhere.

Derek Mahon

The World's Hub

Poor as a Coliseum cat
I lived in an outer suburb with no landmarks
but lime and filth, neither countryside

nor city; that, or was daily packed tight
inside a rattling bus:
and each trip out, each trip back

was a Calvary of hassle and sweat.
Long treks through a miasma of heat
towards even longer dusks

crouched over cards, the road outside
more mud than street, hovels white with dust,
curtains for doors, not a fitting in sight.

And coming from some other suburb
much like this one, an olive-vendor
then the rag-and-bone man ventured past

with goods fallen from the back of a van,
his young face already aged through vices
inculcated by a starving mother . . .

And something within me took root,
at once mine yet not mine,
nourished by the happiness of one

who loves, even if he's not loved back.
And everything was lit up by this love,
however mawkish, despite all odds,

growing up, experience's graduate,
at history's calloused feet.
I was at the world's hub, of all places

here amidst this sad shanty,
these yellow meadows rubbed bald
by the relentless wind,

be it from the warm sea off Fiumicino
or the inland plain where a metropolis vanishes
into hovels: in this world

over which with row upon row
of small barred windows, the Penitentiary
alone holds sway, a cubist spectre

looming amidst the yellowish smog –
stunted houses and what once
were fields cowering below.

Dustclouds, a myriad scraps
gusts hauled blindly to and fro;
the poor echo-less voices

of the squat women come from
across the Adriatic then over the Sabine mountains
and now camped out here with a swarm

of precociously hard children
in gaudy tattered singlets,
grey and fourth-hand shorts;

African-type suns, fits of rain
turning the streets into mudslides;
those buses on their last wheels or less,

their final terminus
between some pale strips of grass
and an acidic smouldering rubbish tip . . .

it was the world's hub,
however unlikely; at the hub of history
my love for it: and in this

realisation which in order to survive
or flourish was still love, everything was
about to become clear – was, yes,

clear! This ghetto unshielded from the wind,
not Roman, not southern,
not even strictly working class,

it was life as it is lived:
life, and light of life, full to bursting,
not yet pigeonholed 'proletarian'.

Martin Bennett

To a Pope*

Shortly before you died, death turned her gaze
onto someone who was your own age:

* See note on Pope Pius XII, p. 78. [Editor's note]

at twenty, you were a student, he a labourer,
you were rich, aristocratic, he one of the low,
but the same days shed gold for you both
on that ancient Rome which was being spruced up.
I've seen what was left of him, poor Zucchetto.
He was roaming drunk around the Markets
and was hit by a tram coming from San Paolo.
Dragged briefly along the rails between the plane trees,
for some hours he lay there, beneath the wheels
while a small group gathered to stare at him
in silence: it was late; there were few passers-by.
One of those men who exist because you exist,
an old scruffy cop with the face of a thug,
shouted at those who came too close: 'Why don't you
    bugger off!'
Then an ambulance arrived to take him away,
and the people dispersed, leaving the odd shred here and
    there.
The woman who ran the nearby late bar
and knew him told someone who'd just arrived
that Zucchetto'd fallen under a tram and was done for.
You yourself died a few days later: Zucchetto was one
of your vast human and Roman flock,
a wretched drunk, without a family or a bed.
He traipsed about at night, somehow scraping a living
– you knew nothing of him as you knew nothing
of innumerable other creatures like him.
Perhaps it's cruel of me to ask what made
people like Zucchetto unworthy of your love . . .
There are shameful places where mothers and babies
live in age-old dust, in the mud of bygone eras.
And not that far from where you yourself lived
in sight of St Peter's glorious dome,

there's one of those places – Gelsomino –
a hill carved in half by a quarry, and beneath,
between a ditch and some newly-built flats,
a heap of slums, not houses but pigsties.
A sign from you or a word would have been enough
and those sons of yours would have had a house
but you neither gave that sign nor said a word.
It's not as if you were being asked to pardon Marx!
Through life's millennia, a huge wave has kept breaking,
sundering you from him, from his religion
– but in your religion don't you speak of compassion?
Many thousands throughout your pontificate,
under your very eyes, have lived in pens and sties.
Sinning doesn't mean doing evil, and you knew that:
not doing good, that's what sinning means.
How much good you could have done. And you didn't.
A greater sinner than you has never lived.

Jamie McKendrick

LUCIANO ERBA
[b. 1922, Milan]

La Grande Jeanne

It made no difference to la grande Jeanne
whether they were French or English
so long as they had hands
the way she liked them
she lived in the port, her brother
was working with me
in 1943.
When she saw me at Lausanne
walking by in summer clothes
she told me I could save her
and that her world was there, in my hands
and my teeth which had eaten hare in high mountains.
At heart
la grande Jeanne would have liked
to become a respectable lady
she had a hat already
broad, blue, and with three turns of tulle.

Peter Robinson

Festival of Nations

I awake to a coming and going
of overturned bottles
mahogany walls approach
in the darkness night wavers
temples howl at the portholes
like dogs at the moon

it began with Austria
taking the stage, folk dances
performed with hands on hips, and then
the latin sisters, expected to have
more brio or there was far too much
with the Scots
there were at least thoughts of death
thanks to their mournful drone
but Italy
no, Italy's a squire in a coach
with collar up, long sideburns
who halts before an inn sign
between Colorno and Rubiera*
stands everyone a round of drinks
leaves ceaselessly lashing at his two-in-hand
looks forward and behind
keeping things at a distance, behind, far behind,
back to his studies in the seminary
where always there was something that he could not say
but it's not so easy to put all this on
in the middle of the ocean.

Peter Robinson

When I Think of My Mother

I wrote nothing of you after you'd gone
and I've written little since, the long time since.
You only return in dreams of every night
or, daytime, by chance, in the air of via B

---

* Colorno and Rubiera are in Emilia and the setting is derived from Stendhal's
The Charterhouse of Parma. [Translator's note]

after it's snowed and one can breathe;
or in an afternoon light of half-closed blinds
and there's a rustle of large newspapers;
or in some place-name that sticks in the throat.
That's all? I don't accept death, they tell me.
It's true, I don't open your drawers, don't reread
your letters. As if
I were no more than a stone,
a little Johnny heartless?
How much time remains to me still
for learning how to smile and love like you?

1978–83

Peter Robinson

La Vida Es . . .*
(*rereading Parini*)

The municipal bus's cheerful route
the foot unfaltering at corners and stops
the usual crowd, if a woman should smile,
her daring flanks bandaged with cretonne,
so much is enough for the old passenger
to feel himself come back to life a moment
(but a chorus from Verdi or certain light too
through leaves in the Guastalla gardens).

Or should a well-meaning young man say 'Please
do sit down' no, it's not a great evil because
the roles are foreseen and quite clear
the old one indeed takes the seat with pride

---

* From Calderón de la Barca's *La vida es sueño* (Life is a dream).
[Translator's note]

with that rediscovered dignity
in the ballet of customs and habits.

But if it's some yahoo that says 'Do sit down'
or, worse, one of those who would wish
to change the world with knapsack and beard,
the gesture just sounds like a sentence
of death without leave to appeal. My wrinkles,
the passenger says to himself, my white mane,
my burdened-down shoulders have moved
even this pseudo–proletarian.

And for all to return as before
the sun the world the day and illusion
what's needed is that as the vehicle brakes
the big greenish jacket of the bearded man
should have mounted on the flowers of cretonne
in this bus's valley of Jehoshaphat
on its journey, yellow, beneath the chestnut trees.

Peter Robinson

BARTOLO CATTAFI

[1922–1979; b. Barcellona Pozzo di Gotto, Messina]

Door

Bare and humble
offspring of a plant
squared off as God willed
resist them
with every fibre
brace yourself lengthways sideways
daub yourself with a sign of fiery paint
they will come by night
they'll hurl themselves upon you
in an avalanche
howling with outspread wings
with punches kicks and curses
with the heads of rams
the stink of sulphur.

Jamie McKendrick

Haste

I ask myself if it's really that bad
your telling me to hurry up
that you don't want
to involve the zone raised and taut,
beyond the doors of pure
and simple surface,
in the depths, the part
of the vagina
so close to the heart

to your soul.
Between ten to twenty minutes
to reach the boiling point.

Rina Ferrarelli

Olives

Sleek matrons
small novices faces in shadow
sharp-faced little whores
I take off your
veil of cellophane
innermost flesh
fine tissue from oats
to anthracite black
girlfriends with kinky ideas
four directions four-fold capacity
on the landing strips
stone-bearing olives phials
of a very volatile essence
oil in length, width, thickness
caressing and concrete oil
timid forest storms
mushrooms fruits chocolates
roses withered by a gust
smoked
what's left of a smoky sun
snacks scattered on the branches
still up in the air
still de-chlorinated
schoolgirls wrapped in a strong
oleic acid gaily carbolic

veins that pass October
and November in warm places
whoever sees you behind the glass
crowded confused in such a bad way
with false health
and a poisonous taste
might want to go up the ladder again
take you back to the branches
to a multiple fate
to the sky of your flights.

Rina Ferrarelli

A Tree

Here is a tree writ well
in black in green and brown
with its wrinkles
the little leaves of Spring
the birds on its branches
and the insects in procession
the tiny monsters
which worship every part of it
and step by step they eat into it
but not in winter
when they sleep
in the depths of the ink

Brian Cole

Snails

Snails and snails
the best known
are like greyhounds
with clear flesh
neck of a swan
tall elegant with good bearing
The others
small squat dark
Southerners closed
of mind and shell
with hard cells
would even go abroad for half
a lettuce leaf
they become sprinters
they do the thousand metres hurdles
with ever more hurdles
until they die.

Brain Cole

Wingspan

Is it the opening of wings?
It changes; where there is nothing
of microns, of centimetres, of metres.
It depends on the model, the material,
the motive power; the objective, the height to be reached.
Folded again, closed up, angular
under the greenest of garlands, in Eden
a feast for happy moths;

or else under the ice with wreckage, bones
of kings, mammoths, dead flies
deep in the amber of time.
We walked beyond our strength,
often we saw, deep in memory, grieving,
a flock of white rags . . . (hardly
a game, a helping hand, a sham
if on the scene of the desert the fire
cleaves to the skin of its prey
if the frost collects dehumanised names).
A beating of wings up to the vast
cliffs of memory does not take us away
from the shadows that pursue us; the hyena,
the wolf, the vile
angels with their falsely majestic gait.

Brian Cole

Guardian Angel

A cat-house in Tunis, I'd barely
put a foot inside the door
when they asked me was I a sailor? No I said
but I might as well be,
I get around so much. Whoever
gets around that much
takes everything with him, including fever.
Three girls were buzzing around the room –
une Française, from Lille, as it turned out,
an Italian bit, and the third,
an Arab, very swarthy –
from Oran –, the best.

You're sick, you've got a fever,
the eyetie piece informed me
and she seemed to think that the last word.
I asked her how the hell she could tell –
you can see it in your face, she said, you're burning up
and in your eyes, she said, you
can see it everywhere.
You're completely off the wall, I said,
you don't know me from Adam, and anyway,
since when can you tell what goes on
under a person's skin?
But she just brushed my forehead with her palm
and the fever went up ten degrees at least.
Clear out, she said, it's
your health I'm thinking of, I'm
your guardian angel. Well
thanks but no thanks I answered
you can leave me out of all that, so far
you've only made things worse.
I made a move for Khedidja, the girl from Oran –
the angel, who was white as the driven snow,
flushed deep red,
put a big breast
back inside her slip, and hit me
right between the shoulderblades
with these words:
You're digging yourself a grave
with your own two hands.

Alan Jenkins

ANGELO MARIA RIPELLINO
[1923–1978; b. Palermo, Sicily]

'Don't make such a din with the dessert spoons'

Don't make such a din with the dessert spoons
– Scardinelli's still playing in the salon next door.
The cake is decked with weird pinnacles and tiny, festive
    lanterns
but not the smallest crumb will pass his lips.
It's because of that his music is so bitter.

But what the hell – go on, clang away! – The pianist
is always feeding on the same crushed hopes,
the iridescent hues and saccharine tiffs
of a defunct era. And who cares?
The eruption of a stormy fanfare,
a swarm of funereal brass trumpets
will stifle his laments of broken pans,
his stridulating trills.
But still it's good he has his pockets stuffed
with bunches of cherries – to offer them
to the pale blue ladies who still love him.

Jamie McKendrick

'Judith wants to read books by critics'

Judith wants to read books by critics.
It's autumn and what on earth should I advise her?
Meanwhile, friends, I've been knocking back a few
and not one blather-merchant's name will come to mind.
To hold her hands is all I want to do,

and stroke her face of shining plaster
and in an alpine gush of profane gibberish
slump in the sudden welcome of her arms.
And like a wounded swordsman to declare:
Judith, my cinnamon, my turtle dove,
I too was once a critic, a stroppy one at that,
but, thanks be to God, now criticism's dead.

Jamie McKendrick

'Habet Islandia coloris albi ingentes ursos'

Habet Islandia coloris albi ingentes ursos*
and we have the gardener Mentzelius,
small, round, with big boots up to his beret-covered ears,
Mentzelius who, steeped in beer from dawn to dusk,
battered the footpaths with his braggart steps.
His boots bestride the corks, the swollen troll,
his beret over his ears, his piggy eyes hopping
like circus fleas – he swills and quaffs away
his little life of a slimeball clown, the bottle-guzzler,
but at home he keeps a Bible, mildewed, old as Methusalah.

Jamie McKendrick

* Iceland has huge white-coloured bears. [Translator's note]

MARIA LUISA SPAZIANI
[b. 1924, Turin]

March in Rue Mouffetard

Stinking and cheerful, the Mouff descends
through gregorian rhythms and mosque laments.
The geranium pierces the rubble, a windy
backdrop from Algeria wrangles
beyond decrepit roofs, amongst the hundred
eyes in ambush at Contrescarpe.
Dried cod, arquebuses, incunabula,
seal's lard, damasks, cymbals
over the paprika and cinnamon river.
At dusk, a subtle fever
perturbs the labyrinth, it calls
the anthill to the fire. Quiet, Patriarchs
with daggers in deep clay necropolises
engrave the millennia
on the tender moon.

At night, black rumbas stir
the derelict refuge of Verlaine.

Peter Robinson

'Rome has a thousand fountains, and in May they sing'

Rome has a thousand fountains, and in May they sing
and gurgle, pontificate and thunder
as if the not too distant sea were bursting
through their secret mouths. Goddesses, titans,

river divinities, turtles
and angels and shells and cornucopias.
Maybe the truth, always suppressed,
is that every street, piazza or alleyway,
even the ones with palaces, herms and obelisks
and cathedrals and stadiums, is an incredibly fragile
crust, a sargasso sea
just on the verge of coming undone and giving up.
The sea is there, the sea is here, boiling furiously
out from these siren-voiced peepholes.
It calls to the ancient country, it resounds,
it rustles with pearls and jellyfish,
it announces the reign of the Mothers, by some obscure
    fate,
it readies its depths,
its music-filled grottoes, its archways
of shadow and triumph.

Beverly Allen

'Tender heart, hairy muscle'

Tender heart, hairy muscle,
are you strong enough to cry to the wind
that happy was the day (not yet born)
when, crazed, down from the Alpine
slopes descended uncontested the bellowing
herd of elephants as they crushed
the woods sacred to your gods
with blithe apocalypse? (How many centuries
did it take to make my heart
such a lustrous museum?) Now the Ottokar hoards
are encamped in the shade

of the Forums and at night on the Parian marble whiteness
they dance up dusty caracallas
drunk with barbarous rhythms. The moon
rises from the Aventine and bathes everything
in her fairy-tale milk, serene,

nor has any edict informed her as yet
that undoubtedly she remains a heavenly body, but,
as a goddess, she's done for.

Beverly Allen

GIOVANNI GIUDICE
[b. 1924, Le Grazie, La Spezia]

Change Your Job

You can't change your life, so why not change firms?
The workplace (don't try to shirk it)
amounts to more than half your soul. And consider
how many changes you'd have in return!

Other faces, other roads on route to work
– which is almost as good as having changed towns,
as having a life before you. Then you'll learn
a whole new jargon among your fellow slaves:

it'll take two months to see how pointless that is.
And then new bosses, new bunches of frayed nerves
duly noted by your supervisors.
You'll come across new products and a brand new scale

to measure good and bad by – and lastly you
yourself: they'll all refer to *you* as new.
To far-off friends you can announce your news:
'I'm writing this to let you know I'm now . . .'

Jamie McKendrick

'Why do we dress'

Why do we dress
the dead as though they were alive?
How much more chaste and just is
the nakedness of bodies confronted by
their final throwing off of flesh!

[137]

But we mask them like this
and cover up the felled bones so they can fake
the supine state of their catharsis.

Jamie McKendrick

Description of My Death

Since it was now only a question of hours
and there was a new law that death should be no burden,
the request had already arrived to present myself
directly at the place where they meant to bury me.
It was an important event but nothing too serious.
It fell to my wife herself to tell me to get ready.

I was like a child being taken to the dentist
who they have to calm down: Be a man, it's nothing.
Determined to conform, I manfully put on
a decent suit and a serene expression.
I had some difficulty swallowing as I asked: Anything
    else?
I was the same as I am now only a bit greyer and taller.

We went by foot to the place
that wasn't quite as I'd envisaged it
but in the village next to my own village,
on two coastal terraces facing west.
Lovely sunshine – not too hot – and only a few people.
In charge was a lady who seemed to be expecting me.

In your own good time, she smiled a shade officiously,
please make your way over there – where the coffin was
    ready,
laid on its side on the ground, of the finest wood,

and in its shadowy emptiness I measured my own height.
I wondered who could have paid for wood of that kind
perhaps a sign of respect from my City or the State.

In the same reddish wood there was also a device
to lower me into the coffin that would do for me.
It'll be over in no time, the lady assured me.
My wife was alert as someone doing the shopping.
Inside was some kind of garrotte or gibbet
to break my neck with a click when it shut.

I knew I was duty bound not to feel any fear.
So after debating the cost I found the excuse of my hair,
asking if they were intending to shave me
like someone I'd seen operated on to no avail.
The woman shook her head: There's really
nothing to be scared of. Don't be such a baby.

Perhaps because I was weeping. But then I said: Enough!
Whoever wants to can foot the bill. I'm sorry for any
    trouble.
I left the place and went back down the street.
Who cares if it was only a question of hours.
There was a lovely sun and I wanted to live my death.
To die my life did not come naturally.

Jamie McKendrick

AMELIA ROSSELLI

[*1930–1996; b. Paris, France*]

from War Variations

I was, I flew, I fell trembling into the
arms of God, and may this last sigh
be my whole being, and may the wave reward,
held in difficult union, my blood,
and from that supreme deceit may death
become vermilion be given back to me, and I
who from the passionate brawls of my comrades plucked
that longing for death
will enjoy, finally – the age of reason;
and may all the white flowers along the shore, and
all the weight of God
beat upon my prisons.

*

so that I may not fly, as long as you do not
fall, as long as the light become a whole
universe, that I may sleep, in the injured goodbye.
And may your playful Bridegroom's outfit
cover you, may it be like the Only Supper for
Saints, your sighing without sleeping pills. There's no light
without glory, and there is no hell
without defamation. The dry horizon
is a play of shadows: don't follow it, don't
throw the stone in the water, – that everything
may make do by itself, even in agonizing silence.

Lucia Re and Paul Vangelisti

Sea of Need, Cassandra

　　　　　　　　Sea of need, Cassandra
of the instinctive blue eyes my tranquil captivity
is an oh so sweet oh so implacable reversal of fate.
With sadness I divine in the eyes of the prophet
a medal that reverses at a man's touch. O Cassandra
your eye-sockets are my favoured cell of resignation
and your lips don't mouth other torments than
those you cannot know elsewhere unless in this
most fragile thinking of mine.

Peter Robinson and Emmanuela Tandello

Snowflakes

They look like tiny celebrating insects
a swarm of shrill engines,
pain splintered in wearying attentions
and mustering of bravado.

It's snowing outside; and all this resembles
a youthful fit of crying
if it weren't that now the tears are dry
like the snowflakes.

An expert in meteorological matters
would call it a falling in love
but me, an expert in these things
I'd say perhaps that it's

an ambush!

Peter Robinson and Emmanuela Tandello

EDOARDO SANGUINETI
[*b. 1930, Genoa*]

from Purgatory of Hell

10

This is the cat with the boots, this is the peace of Barcelona
between Charles V and Clemente VII, this is the locomotive,
    the flowery peach tree,
the sea-horse: but if you turn the sheet, Alexander,
you will see money:

these are Jove's satellites, this is the Autostrada del Sole,
this is the square blackboard, this is the first volume
of the Poetae Latini Aevi Carolini, these are the shoes,
these are the lies, this is the School of Athens,
this is butter, this is the picture-card that arrived from
    Finland today,
this is the masseter muscle, this is childbirth:
but if you turn over the page, Alexander,
you'll see money:

and this is the money,
these are the generals with their machine-guns,
these are the cemeteries with their tombs,
and these are the savings banks with their safes,
these are the history books with their histories,
but if you turn over the page, Alexander,
you see nothing.

G. Singh

'Imagine an image of me, cut back by you'

Imagine an image of me, cut back by you, wrenched,
   re-structured, from the odds
and sods of my ego, in this re-stirrable porridge of some
   thirteen thousand days
in round figures (one instance might be a hand being
   wrung, out of focus, in hotel-corridor
gloom, in 54, in Vicenza, a hunch-backed porter
   somewhere by), rummaging,
almost at random, in the knick-knacks crammed in your
   head (for another example,
try the pure white phlebolite – worth the X-ray plate – in
   my bladder, the sign of my self-petrification, and, get
                                     this,
of our being reduced to a solidarity of solid concretions):
   (you can confuse our surgical scannings
and so join us in conjugatory cement):
                        and imagine the boundless number
of troubled permutations opened up (as with an
   uncheckable song-lyrics-writer, as with a shimmery
scarab
kaleidoscope), which multiply us, therefore, the two of us,
   via complicated crossings
and equivocal shifts:
and imagine that you think out for me, try and try again,
   afterwards
one last word (to define me, finish me off):
       (to make for us here, at two points, one stop):

Peter Hainsworth

GIOVANNI RABONI
[b. 1932, Milan]

Requiem

Poor dead people of Lombardy
buried like heaps of roots
in a soaked earth.

      I was thinking
of the girl who died of the Spanish influenza
in '17 (and even this year fresh flowers
on her tomb); of Crespi
killed by the robbers, they say, while returning
from Milan to Saronno (but perhaps
he shot himself with a carbine: which is
what I have believed for years: but now I'm not sure),

of my great-great-grandfather, I.R. prefect
and an admirer of Maria Teresa, and still a member
of her wet cadastre,

of my dead people
seated in straw chairs, with their
transparent hands stretched towards the fire.

G. Singh

My Daughter's Birthday

With wild compunction let the three
candles be lit.
The two sword-fighting confederates, let them leap
on the lids with crashes, the one

reaching six and a half, the other just five
and me thirty-four, and their mum thirty-two
and grandma, if I'm not mistaken, sixty-eight.
This scene won't be repeated.
The scene doesn't come differently portrayed.
And if anybody feels themselves exiled
or comes out with a grudge to some percentage
speak beforehand or tomorrow.
Accept, little witch of marzipan, our diffident tenderness.
Let follow haphazard squeals
from leaden wagons, bursts of machine-gun fire . . .

Peter Robinson

BIANCAMARIA FRABOTTA
[*b. 1946, Rome*]

'Fifties Childhood

When the grass grows there and the city
renounces its noise
a railway line dies. In the outskirts
where sparse houses continue alone
and pungent fennel abandons itself
                                        to the sun
the tram is remembered by few.
Soon the men from the council
will come and lift onto the pavement
this still flourishing plough.

Peter Robinson

ROSSANA OMBRES
[b. 1931, Turin]

Meadow Bug

Aluqa, the demon who swims underwater in streams,
tries to get swallowed by someone
and to stick to small boys' feet and to the paws
of peaceful animals,
concealed himself
between the prophet's right great toe
and the leather strip of his sandal.

The prophet carried him on his foot
wandering between fat and lean
until the time when he arrived
in the middle of the stars, as it was written.
The middle of the stars is a place
where your knees never get tired
and clothes never get soiled.

There Aluqa was immediately discovered
by his color: only the demon of water
had a receding color, the base
color of anguish.

When he fell back into a pond, Aluqa
was mistaken for a meadow bug
and swallowed by an old she-frog.

Ruth Feldman

Embalmer

There is an embalmer who operates
with one of Madonna Gioconda's hairpins;
in place of blood and nerve ganglions,
in the small sacs of dried-up artery
he puts muslin lace, sea-sponge and sawdust of bones
of the harlot Magdalen.

He uses tanned marmot-gut for stitches.
He is accompanied by a blind dog.
And by a parrot that stammers apologies for the relatives
of the one who's being fêted.

Today he will attempt his daily embalming
with a nice creature called Eleazar:
kings and governors have followed Eleazar
without his ever having used
madder roots or laurel leaves
and today Eleazar will invoke Avzhia, angel of presence.

The dog already turns its putrefied eyes
to where it thinks it hears a giant nightingale
extricate itself from a thicket.

Ruth Feldman

PATRIZIA CAVALLI
[*b. 1947, Todi*]

'Before when you left you would always forget'

Before when you left you would always forget
your perfume, your best handkerchief,
your new pants, your gifts for friends,
your gloves, your boots and your umbrella.
This time you left
a pair of Puerto-Rico-yellow
underpants.

Judith Baumel

'I have no seed to spread over the world'

I have no seed to spread over the world
I can't flood urinals or
mattresses. My meager woman's seed
is too little to offend. What can I
leave in the streets, in houses,
in unfertilized bellies? Words
far too many
but they already don't resemble me
they've forgotten the anger
and the curse, they've become young ladies
with slightly bad reputations perhaps
but still young ladies.

Robert McCracken

'The Moroccans with the carpets'

The Moroccans with the carpets
seem like saints
but they're salesmen.

Kenneth Koch

'But first one must free oneself'

But first one must free oneself
of the precise greed that produces us,
that produces me sitting
in the corner of a bar
waiting with clerical passion
for the exact moment when
the little azure fires of the eyes
opposite, of the eyes acclimatized
to risk, the trajectory precalculated,
will demand a blush
from my face. And will obtain a blush.

Robert McCracken and Patrizia Cavalli

GIANNI D'ELIA
[*b. 1953, Pesaro*]

Just So, One Day

Just so, one day, travelling with the days,
it approaches you, in flashes, the idea
as flesh and blood, as the physical presence
of someone you've not seen in years . . .

And it's standing at a bar to sip, with pallid
nodded salute, its expresso – it disappears . . .
And it's got a bag of records, and hasn't shaved
for three days; and, *in the morning*, off it goes . . .

Travelling with the days . . . and it hits you,
and for stretches you forget it, you recall
lightning-struck in a six-syllable line the events
of one summer, *there*, at first dawns – and mixed

in the crowd with irritations, with vanities, truths . . .

Peter Robinson

from Lament for the Old Olivetti

I was christened, you know, by the poet Fortini
(at that time contract inventor for Olivetti)
a brave, clever, and moody man. Newborn

serial-numbered star in the heavens – *Lettera* 32 as it says
in its own clear syllables
on the metal of my sky,
your hand against the green enamel
has worn it pale with years of inspired frenzy.

Tapping me through your winter,
rewriting for hours and hours,
were you slowly becoming yourself,

since that day when, obsessed,
you took me from your father's study?

Michael Donaghy

Voyeur

Those images that turn you on
are they not the hardest, the most focussed,
if they sell like hot cakes here in Moscow and elsewhere
in rubles, yen, dollars, and at the live

sex show of the soft
impaled slots and crazed cocks where,
running on film and tape,
orgasms shudder,

obscene, badly dubbed orgies, yobs and tarts,
long steady zooms in slow-mo
of full mouths splashed
by him who is sucked up gasping by the eyes

making of this performed love
our bodies and dreams?

Michael Donaghy

FRANCO BUFFONI
[b. 1948, Gallarate, Lago Maggiore]

'Aqueducts sewer systems'

Aqueducts sewer systems
Building and paving contractors
General excavation
Declaims the Baldini-Ceccarelli insignia
At the base of your crane.
Safe from commands I watch you climb up again
After lunch, your earring gleaming
For just a second
I collect metal for sculpting, a sectioned
Orange, and you're a pianist on sheet-iron
An artist of the waltz of marble blocks.

Michael Palma

'Who knows what men have in the basement'

Who knows what men have in the basement,
Their little secrets
Among the bottles of wine an old porno tape
The cigarettes they don't touch any more,
The dessert fork from their daughter's
Wedding-broken in pieces.

Michael Palma

'If you don't know what it means in English to maroon'

If you don't know what it means in English to maroon
Think of a runaway black slave
He's a maroon
And through one of those semantic
Conversions that are the jewel of languages
To maroon someone
Means on the contrary actively to abandon him
Especially on an island. A desert island.
The verb as is clear goes back to the eighteenth century
And the classic example which is equally clear
Cites Jan Svilt, homosexual sailor marooned.
The verb is regular.

Michael Palma

ANDREA GIBELLINI
[*b. 1965, Sassuolo*]

Bering's Bones

Ice, nothing but stretches of ice,
the pallor of sea and fierce wonder of the wind.
– Everything negated now, plainly.

Detaching delicately, they fall like half-dead leaves,
eternal in this dreadful nightmare season.
A dark sea lion, a lukewarm day . . .

N. S. Thompson

Four Landscapes

I

An evening vast, like the last on earth,
over a plain washed by a sun deranged,
growing dark behind the straight lines of houses.
Lights shine towards the city and the pines
like rivers in the night,
denying shadows with their beams;
a slow dying like red leaves from a tree.

In the sun's eternal fire a little springtime blue is left,

the absurd paradise of a cruel sea.

II

It is better to be a salamander resisting
the flames with an indifferent look

than an otter absorbed in the turbulent waters,
now the river flows with mud.
A marmot whistles and has the last word of remaining
   sound.

III

All the hubbub is over–
the Cathedral's lions are lifeless in the unfrequented
   shadow.
Near the shore on the bay of Scardovari, the house
planted like a golden autumn leaf
on the border of Enulla here, land next to water
and the building's unmoving stone crumbling in the middle
of a lake (or cold river, even?), the tall grass
greenish and the sky blue as water

with no bounds at all.

IV

The road to the sea, morning rain
on the Adriatic,
strong sea air and green water filling you,
two black dogs frisking on the beach like people
in love, and the branches underfoot, stones,
strips of seaweed, the large boat laid up, not at anchor
on the shipyard quay, its dark wood crumbling
like a storm that collapses

when the first sun rouses summer.

N. S. Thompson

ANTONELLA ANEDDA
[*b. 1955, Rome*]

'To unearth the reason for a verb'

To unearth the reason for a verb
because the truth is it's not time yet
and we don't know whether to rush forwards or take flight.

Make it evening, say an evening in December,
the tea-chests levered up on chocks for removal.
Give form to the darkness
whilst the cooking flares against the wall.

These are the nights of Western peace
and flying in their rays are the cramped biographies,
the berry-dark portraits, the scroll of names.

A different quietness shields us on one side
like a marine weight wrapped in jute
and folded carefully, with desperation.

Jamie McKendrick

Earth

Round, frozen in its oceans, transparent
like a cell under the microscope
or horizontal with mountains planted firmly above fields
with the tongue of rivers and the stretched out sea.

Every now and then I have an inkling of vertigo:
we're turning faster. Asleep, I cry out 'I'm falling'
and then I feel space, blackness, the stars at the nape of my
    neck,

fear which vomits forth a thousand spheres.

'Oh that would be hell' you say and doze off.
So I meditate on hell. It's enough if the curtain's weight
tugs the rings along the glass . . . with precision I see
the marching of a line of ants, the vast starry night.

I try to take hold of hell by its border
(a strip of black, emptiness, fear)
to make it whirl in the courtyard as the fir-tree does in the
    sky
to become the insect that I've always been:
that's born and forgets itself in the air.

Jamie McKendrick

September 2001. Maddalena Archipelago, Island of S. Stefano

This small island riven underwater by U.S. submarines,
where my great-grandfather planted citrus fruits and vines,
built cowsheds and brought ten cows from the mainland.
Their trembling hoofs on the boat, the wind on their backs
only struck till then by rain from the north.
They're still there, horns mingled with the sand,
deep-rooted skeletons, close up to the rocks, no longer
    afraid,
no longer distinguishing pasture from sea.

Jamie McKendrick

VALERIO MAGRELLI

[b. 1957, Rome]

The Tic

Gestures that go astray
appeal to me – the one
who trips up or upturns
a glass of . . . the one who forgets,
is miles away, the sentry
with the insubordinate eyelid
– my heart goes out
to all of them, all who betray
the unmistakeable
whirr and clunk
of the bust contraption.
Things that work are muffled
and mute – their parts just move.
Here instead the gadgetry,
the mesh of cogs, has given up
the ghost – a bit sticks out,
breaks off, declares itself.
Inside something throbs.

Jamie McKendrick

The Vanishing Point

Which is the lefthand side of the word?
How does it move about in space?
Where does it cast its shadow
(and can a word cast shadow)?
How can it be observed from behind

or set against the recession of space?
I should like to render in poetry
the equivalent of perspective in painting.
To give a poem the depth of a rabbit
escaping through fields and make it
distant whilst already
it speeds away from the one who's watching
and veers towards the frame
becoming smaller all the time
yet never moving an inch.
The countryside observes
and disposes itself around the creature,
around a point that's vanishing.

Jamie McKendrick

The Embrace

As you lie beside me I edge closer
taking sleep from your lips
as one wick draws flame from another.
And two night-lights are lit
as the flame passes
between us. But as it passes
the boiler in the basement shudders:
down there a fossil nature burns,
down in the depths prehistory's
sunken fermented peats blaze up
and slither through my radiator.
Wreathed in a dark halo of oil,
the bedroom is a close nest
heated by organic deposits,
by log pyres, leafmash, seething resins . . .

And we are the wicks, the two tongues
flickering on that single Palaeozoic torch.

Jamie McKendrick

They Talk

All around there's such silence one can almost hear
the clink of a teaspoon falling in Finland.
J. Brodsky

But why's it always behind my walls?
Always there, the voices, always
when night falls
they start to talk. They bark. Or even think
whispering's better. (Whilst I can feel their
words become this thread of air
that chills me and chokes me and breaks
my sleep up.) At the polar circle's brink
a couple wept together in their room,
beyond a wall they wept
– its luminous membrane
tender as a drumskin
or an eardrum.
(Whilst I resounded – the sound-box
of their story.) Till they started in on
the roof at my place, the whole thing, the guttering,
battering away at the front, the back,
the top, the bottom, always battering
and chattering away together only when I slept,
only because I slept,
only because I was always
the sound-box
of their stories.

Jamie McKendrick

Aperçu

Only the insane excrescence.
Osip Mandelstam

The solitary worm, the parasite,
the scrounger and the saprophyte,
and cancer, all derive from organisms
that, like Western music,
brood their own end.
First, the gemmation
of timid dissonances, then, the metastases
that invade and disintegrate sound's body:
wondrous decay, orchard
of death. It is the history of a tonal catastrophe,
arhythmic cells, superfetations,
in other words, the Hijacker (for cancer
always hijacks its carrier).
Behold the earth, this hapless aircraft
held hostage by an armed passenger.

Anthony Molina

Acknowledgements

The editor and publishers gratefully acknowledge permission to reprint copyright material in this book as follows:

ANTONELLA ANEDDA: 'To unearth . . .', 'Earth' and 'September 2001', translated by Jamie McKendrick. GIORGIO BASSANI: 'Salute to Rome', translated by Peter Robinson, from *The Great Friend and Other Translated Poems*, edited by Peter Robinson (Worple Press, 2002); 'Towards Ferrara', translated by Jamie McKendrick. ATTILO BERTOLUCCI: 'Wind', 'October Night', 'The Years', 'The Ants' and 'Portrait of a Sick Man' from *Selected Poems*, translated by Charles Tomlinson (Bloodaxe Books, 1993). FRANCO BUFFONI: 'Aqueducts sewer systems', 'Who knows what men have in the basement', 'If you don't know what it means . . .' from *The Shadow of Mount Rosa: Selected Poems of Franco Buffoni*, translated by Michael Palma (Gravida Publications). DINO CAMPANA: 'Woman from Genoa' and 'Whore with Iron-Grey Eyes' from *Orphic Songs*, translated by I. L. Salomon (October House, 1968). GIORGIO CAPRONI: 'For Her', published by permission of Christopher Reid; 'Ottone's its name', translated by Jamie McKendrick; 'After the News', published by permission of Peter Robinson. VINCENZO CARDARELLI: 'Dawn' and 'Lament', published by permission of Michael O'Neill. BARTOLO CATTAFI: 'Door', translated by Jamie McKendrick; 'Haste' and 'Olives', translated by Rita Ferrarelli, from *Modern Poetry in Translation: Contemporary Italian Poetry*, edited by Luca Guerneri (MPT Books/King's College London, 1999); 'A Tree', 'Snails' and 'Wingspan' from *Anthracite*, translated by Brian Cole (Arc Publications, 2000); 'The Good Angel', translated by Alan Jenkins, from *In the Hot-house* by Alan Jenkins (Chatto & Windus, 1988). PATRIZIA CAVALLI: 'Before you left . . .', translated by Judith Baumel', 'I have no seed . . .', translated by Robert McCracken, 'The Moroccans with the carpets', translated by Kenneth Koch, and 'But first one must free oneself', translated by Robert McCracken and Patrizia Cavalli, from *New Italian Poets*, edited by Dana Gioia (Story Line Press, 1991). GABRIELE D'ANNUNZIO: 'The Shepherds' and 'The Mouth of the Arno' from *Italian Landscape Poems*, translated by Alistair Elliot (Bloodaxe Books, 1993); 'The Seahorse', published by permission of Simon Carnell. GIANNI D'ELIA: 'Just So, One Day', published by permission of Peter Robinson; from 'Lament for the Old Olivetti' and 'Voyeur', translated by Michael Donaghy. LUCIANO ERBA: 'La Grande Jeanne', published by permission of Peter Robinson; 'When I Think of my Mother' and 'La Vida Es . . .', translated by Peter Robinson, from *The Great Friend and Other Translated Poems*, edited by Peter Robinson (Worple Press, 2002). FRANCO FORTINO: 'Letter', translated by Jamie McKendrick; 'The

Animal', 'Genre Theory' and 'Reading a Poem', published by permission of
Marcus Perryman and Peter Robinson; 'The Hour of Vile Deeds' and
'Translating Brecht' from *Summer Is Not All: Selected Poems*, translated by Paul
Lawson (Carcanet Press, 1992). BIANCA MARIA FRABOTTA: 'Fifties Childhood',
published by permission of Peter Robinson. ALFONSO GATTO: 'They Could Call
You Dead' and 'Anniversary', translated by G. Singh, from *Contemporary Italian
Verse* (London Magazine Editions, 1968). ANDREA GIBELLINI: 'Bering's Bones'
and 'Four Landscapes', published by permission of N. S. Thompson. GIOVANNI
GIUDICE: 'Change Your Job', 'Why do we dress' and 'Description of My Death',
translated by Jamie McKendrick. CORRADO GOVONI: 'The Tapping' and 'Fields
and Clouds' from *The Blue Moustache: Italian Futurist Poets*, edited by Felix
Stefanile (Carcanet Press, 1981). GUIDO GOZZANO: 'Eulogy of Ancillary
Amours', 'Cocotte' and 'The Good Companion' from *The Colloquies*, translated
by J. G. Nichols (Carcanet Press, 1987). PRIMO LEVI: 'Reveille', 'For Adolf
Eichmann', 'Shemà' and 'August' from *Collected Poems*, translated by Ruth
Feldman and Brian Swann (Faber and Faber, 1992). MARIO LUZI: 'Night Cleans
the Mind' and 'Year', translated by Jamie McKendrick. VALERIO MAGRELLI:
'The Tic', 'The Vanishing Point', 'The Embrace' and 'They Talk', translated by
Jamie McKendrick; 'Apercu' from *The Contagion of Matter*, translated by Antony
Molino (Holmes & Meier Publishing, 2000). GESUALDO MANZELLA-FRONTINI:
'The Anatomy Room' from *The Blue Moustache: Italian Futurist Poets*, edited by
Felix Stefanile (Carcanet Press, 1981). FILIPPO TOMMASO MARINETTI: 'The
Futurist Aviator Speaks to his Father' from *The Blue Moustache: Italian Futurist
Poets*, edited by Felix Stefanile (Carcanet Press, 1981). EUGENIO MONTALE:
'Don't ask us . . .' and lines from 'Motets' from *Collected Poems 1920–1954*,
translated by Jonathan Galassi (Carcanet Press, 1999); from 'Mediterranean'
and 'My Muse', translated by Jamie McKendrick; 'In the Void', published by
permission of Simon Carnell and Erica Segre; 'The Coastguard House', from
Imitations by Robert Lowell (Faber and Faber); 'Eastbourne', published by
permission of Christopher Reid; 'En Route to Vienna', 'From the Train' and
'Two Venetian Pieces', published by permission of Eamon Grennan; 'The
Storm', published by permission of Tom Paulin; 'The Eel', published by
permission of Paul Muldoon, from *Moy Sand and Gravel* by Paul Muldoon
(Faber and Faber, 2004); from 'Xenia I and II', 'In the Smoke' and 'Late at
Night' from *Poems: Montale*, edited by Harry Thomas (Penguin Modern
Classics, 2002). ROSSANA OMBRES: 'Meadow Bug' and 'Embalmer', translated
by Ruth Feldman, from *New Italian Poets*, edited by Dana Gioia (Story Line
Press, 1991). GIORGIO ORELLI: 'In the Family Circle', published by permission
of Peter Robinson; 'Rhine Eels', translated by Jamie McKendrick. PIER PAOLO
PASOLINI: from 'Gramsci's Ashes', translated by Derek Mahon, from *Collected
Poems* by Derek Mahon (The Gallery Press, 1999); 'The World's Hub',
translated by Martin Bennet, from *Modern Poetry in Translation: Contemporary
Italian Poetry*, edited by Luca Guerneri (MPT Books/King's College London,
1999); 'To a Pope', translated by Jamie McKendrick. CESARE PAVESE: 'The

Paper Smokers' and 'The Country Whore', published by permission of Duncan Bush; 'Dina Thinking', 'Two Cigarettes' and 'Death will come . . .' from *Disaffections*, translated by Geoffrey Brock (Copper Canyon Press/Carcanet Press; forthcoming). SANDRO PENNA: 'Country Cemetary', 'Homeward Bound . . .', 'It was in . . .', 'Graveyard lights . . .', 'How difficult, you know', 'For Eugenio Montale' and 'We set out for summer's . . .' from *Remember Me, God of Love*, translated by Blake Robinson (Carcanet Press); 'I have come down . . .', translated by Jamie McKendrick. SALVATORE QUASIMODO: 'Deadwater', 'And Suddenly It's Evening' and 'How Long the Night' from *Complete Poems*, translated by Jack Bevan (Anvil Press Poetry, 1997); 'Elegy', translated by Martin Bennet, and 'Man of My Time', translated by Geoff Page and Loredana Nardi-Ford, from *Modern Poetry in Translation: Contemporary Italian Poetry*, edited by Luca Guerneri (MPT Books/King's College London, 1999); 'On the Branches of Willows' published by permission of Bernard O'Donoghue; 'In a Remote City' and 'Footfall', published by permission of Simon Carnell and Erica Segre; 'The Soldiers Cry at Night', translated by Edwin Morgan. GIOVANNI RABONI: 'Requiem', translated by G. Singh, from *Contemporary Italian Verse* (London Magazine Editions, 1968); 'My Daughter's Birthday', translated by Peter Robinson, from *The Great Friend And Other Translated Poems*, edited by Peter Robinson (Worple Press, 2002). ANGELO MARIA RIPELLINO: 'Don't make . . .', 'Judith wants . . .' and 'Habet Islandia . . .', translated by Jamie McKendrick. NELO RISI: 'Italy' and 'The TV News', translated by Jamie McKendrick. AMELIA ROSSELLI: 'Sea of Need, Cassandra', published by permission of Peter Robinson and Emmanuela Tandelo; 'Snowflakes', translated by Peter Robinson and Emmanuela Tandelo, in *The Great Friens and Other Translated Poems*, edited by Peter Robinson (Worple Press, 2002); from 'War Variations' in *War Variations* (Sun and Moon Classics), translated by Lucia Re Vangelista and Paul Vangelisti (Consortium Book Sales and Distribution, 1999). UMBERTO SABA: 'A Siren', translated by Derek Mahon, from *Derek Mahon: Collected Poems* (The Gallery Press, 1999); 'Ulysses', published by permission of Robert Chandler; 'Woman', translated by Peter Robinson, from *The Great Friend and Other Translated Poems*, edited by Peter Robinson (Worple Press, 2002); 'The Goat', 'The Pig' and 'Thirteenth Match', published by permission of Simon Carnell; 'Caffe Tergeste', translated by Jamie McKendrick; 'A Memory' and 'February Evening', published by permission of Geoffrey Brock. EDOARDO SANGUINETI: from 'Purgatory in Hell', translated by G. Singh (London Magazine Editions, 1968); 'Imagine an image . . .', published by permission of Peter Hainsworth. CAMILLO SBARBERO: 'Father, even if you were not' and 'Hush, soul. These are the abject', published by permission of Christopher Reid. VITTORIO SERENI: from 'Algerian Diary' (1, 6), 'A Dream' and 'Saba' from *Selected Poems of Vittorio Sereni*, translated by Peter Robinson and Marcus Perryman (Anvil Press Poetry, 1990); from 'Algerian Diary' (9), published by permission of Tom Paulin. LEONARDO SINISGALLI: 'Dog Flies', 'My Mother' and 'The Canaries', translated by Jamie McKendrick.

MARIA LUISA SPAZIANI: 'March in Rue Mouffetard', published by permission of Peter Robinson; 'Rome has a thousand fountains . . .' and 'Tender heart, hairy muscle', translated by Beverly Allen, from *New Italian Poets*, edited by Dana Gioia (Story Line Press, 1991). GIUSEPPE UNGARETTI: 'Agony', 'Watch', 'I am Alive', 'In Memorium', 'Levant' and 'My Rivers' from *Selected Poems*, translated by Patrick Creagh (Penguin Modern European Poets, 1971); 'Chiaroscuro', translated by Peter Robinson and Marcus Perryman, from *The Great Friend and Other Translated Poems*, edited by Peter Robinson (Worple Press, 2002); 'On the Edge of Sleep', published by permission of Marcus Perryman and Peter Robinson; 'Contrite', translated by Hugh MacDiarmid; 'Last Quarter', published by permission of Simon Carnell and Erica Segre; 'The Flash of the Mouth' from *Selected Poems*, from *Selected Poems*, translated by Andrew Frisardi (Carcanet Press, 2003). ANDREA ZANZOTTO: 'Where Are They?' and 'For Eugenio Montale on His Eightieth Birthday' from *Peasant's Wake for Fellini's Casanova and Other Poems*, translated by John P. Welle and Ruth Feldman (University of Illinois Press, 1997).

Index of Poets